Shotgun for Hire

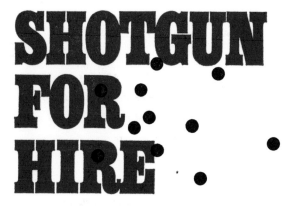

SHOTGUN FOR HIRE

The Story of "Deacon" Jim Miller,
Killer of Pat Garrett

By GLENN SHIRLEY

University of Oklahoma Press : Norman

BY GLENN SHIRLEY

Toughest of Them All (Albuquerque, 1953)

Six-Gun and Silver Star (Albuquerque, 1955)

Law West of Fort Smith: A History of Frontier Justice in the Indian Territory, 1834–1896 (New York, 1957, 1961; Lincoln, 1968)

Pawnee Bill: A Biography of Gordon W. Lillie (Albuquerque, 1958; Lincoln, 1965)

Buckskin and Spurs: A Gallery of Frontier Rogues and Heroes (New York, 1958)

Outlaw Queen: The Fantastic True Story of Belle Starr (Derby, Conn., 1960)

Heck Thomas, Frontier Marshal (New York & Philadelphia, 1962)

Born to Kill (Derby, Conn., 1963)

Henry Starr, Last of the Real Badmen (New York, 1965)

Buckskin Joe: The Unique and Vivid Memoirs of Edward Jonathan Hoyt, Hunter-Trapper, Scout, Soldier, Showman, Frontiersman, and Friend of the Indians 1840–1918 (Lincoln, 1966)

Shotgun for Hire: The Story of "Deacon" Jim Miller, Killer of Pat Garrett (Norman, 1970)

INTERNATIONAL STANDARD BOOK NUMBER: 0–8061–0902–5

LIBRARY OF CONGRESS CATALOG CARD NUMBER: 78–108794

Foreword

HE was born to hang. In Jim Miller's own words, "the bullet wasn't made that could kill him."

After they placed the noose around his neck, he calmly took a diamond ring from his finger and directed that it be sent to his wife, then carefully outlined disposition of his other property.

"I'm ready now," he said. "You couldn't kill me otherwise. Let 'er rip!"

The rope on the barn rafter jerked, and Jim Miller was no more. The game manner in which he had faced death settled nothing. Some cited it as proof that he was absolutely without fear; others thought it showed how inhuman he really was.

He had murdered his first victims, his own grandfather and grandmother, when he was eight. By the time he was forty-three, the year he was hanged, fifty-one persons had died by his gun. That was Miller's claim. I find only eighteen victims, with seven of these alleged, not proven.

The "sheepherders" and "nesters" mentioned by Miller can be dismissed as vague and generalized.

Despite these discrepancies, Miller was easily the most dangerous man in the Southwest; compared to him, the notorious John Wesley Hardin and Billy the Kid were merely sensational gunfighters. He was not a typical outlaw in the tradition of Sam Bass or the others of that kind who infested Texas, Oklahoma, and New Mexico until the early 1900's. He always dressed well. He was intelligent, charming, and even somewhat handsome. He never drank, cursed, or chewed; he showed up at church on Sundays and was almost prudish in his contact with women. As Dee Harkey, the old-time Western lawman, said, "he was what you would call a moral man unless you knew his avocation. He was just a killer and seemed to love it. He would kill any man for money."

His shotgun was for hire—at fifty, one hundred, or two thousand dollars per head. And he made no secret of it.

Yet the Miller story has never been fully told; his actual victims have never been tabulated. This is an attempt to do both.

GLENN SHIRLEY

Stillwater, Oklahoma

Contents

Illustrations

Shotgun for Hire

1. Stranger in a Black Coat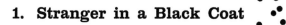

JIM MILLER could feel the heavy cloud of curiosity that hung over Pecos that August afternoon in 1891. The town had the appearance of having been deserted as business was suspended and citizens took refuge from the blistering heat in the scanty shade of store fronts. The only signs of life were the click of poker chips and occasional gusts of laughter from the bars and gambling dens. Miller was soon aware, however, that every eye was upon him.

Strangers arriving in this raw settlement on the West Texas frontier usually got only brief glances. Dudes in slick city clothes, gamblers in flowered vests getting off the train or stage—these were the usual types. But the slender, long-legged Miller, in his mid-twenties and mounted on a high-stepping big gray, was different.

Bud Thompson recalled: "I was in my saddle shop working on a fancy tooled skirt when I heard the clop-clop of horse hoofs. I looked out and my eyes most popped. I saw this stranger all decked out in a black broadcloth coat, and

3

I asked myself why a young feller wanted to gallivant around in an outfit like that with the temperature hot enough to fry bacon on the stock of a Winchester! He was no saddle bum. He rode too proud for that. And he had a nice smile on his face that made you feel good. Then he looked down and saw me watching him, and our eyes met for a second. Man, those eyes! Pale blue, they was, and so cold looking that goose bumps popped out on my arms. He didn't say anything, just rode on past."

He looked neither right nor left, but from the corners of his unblinking eyes Miller caught the stares that followed on either side. Perspiration broke from the thick brown hair under his broad-brimmed hat, trickled down his roundish, full cheeks, and vanished in the edges of his sweeping, neatly trimmed mustache. Alkali from the sun-scorched street kicked up in little puffs behind his big gray. He knew what these people were thinking.

He swung down in front of Juan's saloon, and the town seemed to come alive. Heads appeared in doors and windows. Quickly he crossed the wooden porch and disappeared through the swinging doors. In the dark coolness of the interior, more curious eyes stared at him as he stepped to the bar and ordered water to wash the trail dust from his throat.

"I locked up my shop," Thompson said, "and skedaddled down to Juan's. As I walked in the door, the stranger was just emptying his glass, and the room had got so quiet you could hear folks talking across the street."

At the bar, a range boss named Hearn and half a dozen cowboys who had ridden in only minutes before put down their whiskey. A tough outfit, headquartered in the Toyah Creek country, they felt duty bound to tree the town each time they visited. Any excuse was sufficient.

Hearn, a man in his thirties, built like a small bull and wearing shirt sleeves cut off at the elbows, stepped up the counter to within a foot of Miller.

"That coat of yours," he said, in a clear, carrying voice, "just naturally makes me sweat."

Miller squinted in disgust at the odor of grime and range dung, and said, "I don't like your smell."

"Take it off," Hearn ordered.

Miller replied, "Go to hell," and Hearn's right hand flashed downward in a movement too quick for the eye to follow. His fingers were around the butt of his .45 when the unexpected happened.

Like the smooth mechanism of a perfect machine, Miller's right hand went under the tail of his coat and an ivory-handled six-shooter seemed to leap against Hearn's belly.

"Drop it!" Miller snapped.

Hearn let his half-drawn weapon fall back in its holster as if it was red-hot. "H-hell's bells," he stuttered, "I was only foolin'."

Miller's expression didn't change. He stepped back slightly, cold blue eyes watching Hearn. "You have a couple of minutes to get out of town and take your fools with you," he said.

Since the muzzle of the weapon was still pointing at his stomach, Hearn nodded to his riders, mutely.

Just sixty seconds later, according to old-timers who were present, the cowboys rode down the street, leaving their boss behind.

"Now," Miller said to Hearn, "you don't really mind me wearing a coat in hot weather, do you? If you ever come back to Pecos to raise hell, I'll have to kill you. I like this town and intend to settle here."

A half-minute later, the range boss rode after his cow-

5

boys. His humiliation was complete, and there is nothing in the records to show that he ever made trouble in Pecos again. When the dust of the departing riders had settled, Miller turned back into the saloon and bought drinks for his fascinated audience, ordering for himself another glass of water.

The story swept about town that afternoon, and everyone sopped it up eagerly. Even Sheriff G. A. "Bud" Frazer, when he heard it, rushed over to the saloon and bought a round of drinks.

By this time, there was a large crowd around Miller, talking and eying his coat. But just why he wore the garment in the August heat, they already had decided, was none of their business.

Frazer was as curious about the coat as anybody else. When another round had been bought and the six or seven men close to Miller moved away, drinking and laughing, the sheriff sidled up to him, sort of cleared his throat, and inquired, confidential-like, "Would you mind telling me, sir, just why you wear a coat in weather like this?"

For a moment those pale eyes went cold. The smile vanished from under Miller's sweeping mustache, causing it to droop. The crowd grew tense and quiet, half expecting to see that ivory-handled six-shooter leap into view again. But the smile returned to his face, and he looked at Frazer.

"This coat, you might say," he answered politely, "is my life insurance. So long as I wear it no harm can come to me."

The crowd relaxed a little. Then Miller continued in the same gentle voice. "You see," he said, "this coat belonged to an old friend of mine. He sheriffed on the border for years without getting a scratch. Claimed it was the coat. Died in bed, he did, with his boots off." Miller paused and

6

stroked the worn and dusty broadcloth. "He gave it to me. I figured it must be lucky."

Frazer looked around and grinned, and everyone went back to drinking and talking. A man had a right to his own superstition, he figured, and that ended the matter. Soon the sheriff and Miller were joking together. Finally they went down to Frazer's office. When they appeared on the street again, Miller wore a deputy's star on the front of his black coat.

Although Frazer didn't know it at the time, he had pinned a badge on the Southwest's first hired gun. This mild-mannered stranger was well on his way to becoming the most dangerous man in Texas, Oklahoma, and New Mexico.

2. Hard Men—A Raw Land

HISTORIANS who have mentioned Miller in other works do not give his full name. He is referred to as "James P." and "J. P." Dee Harkey, the old-time Texas and New Mexico lawman, who, in his book *Mean As Hell*, says Miller was the first man he ever arrested, knew him only as "Jim." A Fort Worth newspaperman who interviewed Miller toward the end of his career claimed his middle initial was "B." and that he was born at Van Buren, Arkansas, on October 24, 1866.

Little is known of his early life except that his family moved to Franklin, Robertson County, Texas, when Jim was a year old. A few years later both parents died. Jim's older sister married a farmer named John Coop, and the boy was sent to live with his grandparents in Coryell County. In 1874, when he was eight, his grandfather and grandmother were found murdered in their home at Evant. Jim was arrested for the double slaying, but never prosecuted. He was placed in the custody of the Coops, who now lived in Coryell County on Plumb Creek, eight miles northwest of Gatesville.

Jim didn't get along with his brother-in-law. Although he was outwardly calm and quiet, the boy possessed a terrible temper, which he fully exercised each time Coop disciplined him. Coop's unkindnesses, real and fancied, became an obsession with Jim. About 9:00 P.M., July 30, 1884, Coop died from a shotgun blast while peacefully sleeping in a bed on his porch.

The trouble between Jim and his brother-in-law was no secret, and again Jim was arrested. He was now seventeen. This time he was indicted and tried for murder at Gatesville.

Miller testified that at the time of the shooting he was attending a camp meeting at Camp Branch, nearly three miles away. His witness was Miss Georgia Large. Miss Large said he had accompanied her to the meeting, that they had sat "side by side in the arbor until the preaching began," but that he had then excused himself and "did not return until the regular service was over and the shouting commenced." Miller was unable to give an account of himself during this period of about forty minutes—time enough, the prosecution insisted, "to ride to the Coop home, fire the load of buckshot into the body of his brother-in-law and return for the preaching and shouting."

Other testimony showed that Miller had ridden a fast horse the night of the meeting; that several days prior to the murder, Jeff Coop, the victim's brother, had made a test run on the same horse from Camp Branch to the Coop home and back, with watches being held at both ends of the ride; and that Miller knew of the ride and to the second how much time would elapse between the start at Camp Branch, arrival at the Coop place, and return to the point of starting.

9

The jury decided Miller had laid his plans accordingly. He was sentenced to life imprisonment. Fate, however, had decreed a far more interesting future for Jim.

His lawyer took the case to the Texas Court of Appeals and won a reversal and an order for a new trial on two points: the court had erred in refusing Miller a requested continuance to permit him to perfect an alibi, and the jury had received "an instruction contrary to law." Years ago, the pre-1909 records of the appeals court were ordered destroyed by the state legislature, but the facts are amply stated in Cause No. 3283, *Miller* v. *State*, *Texas Criminal Appeals*, Volume 18.

By the time the second trial was called, most of the damaging witnesses against Miller had either left the country or "mysteriously disappeared." The case was never retried. It was marked by all the color, action, and intrigue that later characterized his technique—a blast from a shotgun (his favorite weapon for murder), escape on horseback, release on bond if arrested, a capable lawyer for defense, and an alibi.

Miller drifted into San Saba County. When next heard from, he was running with the three Renfro brothers and a man named Bill White. Dee Harkey's oldest brother, Joe, was sheriff, and Dee had just gone to work for him as a deputy. According to Dee, the Renfros were a "bad bunch" and had been making "a roughhouse of the town." Joe had brought one of the brothers back from Magdalena, New Mexico, for stealing a cow in San Saba, and the jury found him guilty. After the trial, one of the jurors stepped into Mitch Johnson's saloon. Bill White was there. Some words were passed, and White "slapped him down." The juror rushed down to the jail demanding White's arrest.

Renfro and some other prisoners had tunneled through

the jail wall the day before, and Dee was guarding the hole to keep the rest from escaping. Joe told Dee he expected to have trouble, so Dee "left Jailer Daugherty in charge of the guarding" and went with his brother. They located the gang in Williams' saloon.

Peeping through the lattice door in front, Joe pointed out White and Jim Miller. The three Renfros were playing pool. Joe ordered Dee to rush Miller, and he would rush White. He told Dee to kill if necessary. Dee charged through the door, but when he stuck his gun in Miller's face, Miller threw up his hands and gasped, "My God, kid, don't kill me!"

Dee took Miller's six-shooter; Joe disarmed White and the Renfros, and they put all five men in jail. The district attorney didn't want to prosecute because Joe had failed to obtain warrants before making the arrests, but the judge ordered the whole gang held for trial because they had been "running over all the officers until Joe was elected sheriff." Dee said the decision had a "wholesome effect," for he had "no further contact with Mr. White," and Miller moved west into McCulloch County.

In McCulloch County, Jim seems to have gambled some, raced horses, and worked as a cowboy for Emanuel "Mannen" (or "Manning") Clements, one of the largest and best-known horse and cattle ranchers in Texas. Clements was brother of the notorious Jim, Gip, and Joe of the famous Taylor-Sutton feud and cousin of John Wesley Hardin of the old DeWitt County clan—all men whose names had often been connected with sudden death.

The Clements family had driven many herds north from Gonzales County during the early 1870's. In July, 1871, in the Indian Territory, Mannen had killed two of his trail hands, Joe and Adolph Shadden, in an argument over their

11

work. He once broke Hardin from the Gonzales jail, and he had taken care of Wes's wife and children after Hardin was captured and sent to prison. In the spring of 1880, Mannen was charged in two cases of "driving stock from its accustomed range" in DeWitt County. The following September, both cases were dismissed for lack of prosecution. He then moved to San Saba, where he lived for a time, and he finally owned places in Runnels and McCulloch counties.

It is not known where Miller met Clements, but possibly it was during his stay at San Saba. In any event, he was on the fall and spring roundups of 1886 and 1887 at the Clements ranch in McCulloch County. Despite his reputation—and Mannen must have known something of the previous record of his new hired hand—Jim found a warm welcome. He rode the range with Clements' son, Mannie, Jr., who became his good friend. They made such frontier towns as Cowboy, Trickham, Paint Rock, and Ballinger. He saw the hills and valleys of the region known as the Hill Country, where Brady Creek, the San Saba, and the north fork of the Concho ran down from the south and west to the Colorado. He even attended some of the country dances with Mannie's shy but pretty sister, Sallie. Jim liked Sallie from the first moment he saw her, and Sallie liked him. After all, he was a well-mannered and handsome young man.

Jim bided his time with Sallie and was careful not to let her family think he was too much interested in her. The Clementses were bred of strong ties and traditions, and in this line Jim had nothing to offer. Although Mannen himself had killed men, he was not a murderer in the style of Jim Miller, and the prospect of having a son-in-law with the habit of disposing of his relatives would have chilled any move on Miller's part toward marriage. But Jim soon had the opportunity to win the undying gratitude of the entire Clements clan.

In 1887, Mannen became candidate for sheriff of the new county of Runnels. It was a heated campaign, and Mannen did little to temper the passions of the opposition. On March 29, while taking a drink in the Senate Saloon at Ballinger, he was shot and killed by City Marshal Joe Townsend.

Later, Townsend was riding home one night from a short trip outside the city when a shotgun blast from the darkness knocked him from the saddle. He survived his wounds, but his left arm had to be amputated. His assailant was never identified. Everybody suspected Jim Miller.

Jim wasn't around to argue the point. He had suddenly dropped from sight. Some said he was visiting his sister in Coryell County, but others claimed he had left his past behind and had gone to southeastern New Mexico. There is evidence that he was around Eddy (Carlsbad) and the Seven Rivers country the next two years, eking out a living at gambling, and he was seen in saloons on the Mexican border. He was still drifting when he rode into Pecos in 1891.

Miller never said why he chose this section of West Texas for a new start. It was a hard land. Countless chronicles painted a picture of its bleakness and sinister desolation.

Captain William Whiting, who commanded the first of several expeditions sent to the region by the United States Army early in 1849 to find a southern trail to California, noted its "monotonous and sombre features, destitute of foliage." Colonel Joseph E. Johnston, leading a similar expedition from San Antonio in June of that year, wrote: "Few places can be found more solitary or that present a more dreary appearance." Lieutenant S. G. French, who accompanied Johnston, commented on the crookedness, steep banks, and bitter waters of the Pecos River, and added: "No tree or bush marks its course. One may stand on its banks and not know the stream is near. The only inhabitants of its waters are catfish. The antelope and wolf alone visit its silent, desolate shores." Lieutenant Nathaniel Michler, arriving with a small party later in the year, saw the river at flood stage "running bank full and a hundred feet wide, a rolling mass of red mud." Antonio de Espejo, who led an expedition to the Pecos in 1583, called it the Río de las Vacas, the "River of Cows," because of the number of dead buffalo he found in the vicinity. Castaño de Sosa, who saw it in 1590, named it Río Salado, "Salt River." The forty-niners, emigrants, and freighters, who crossed it in the decade prior to the Civil War, declared the water was "so gyppy it would give a killdee that just flew over it the diarrhea."

The twenty-foot banks made it nearly impossible to cross at most places, but twenty miles up the river from present Girvin, on a line between Fort Stockton and Crane, the banks sloped down to the water. This crossing, called the Horsehead, became the funnel point for numerous southwestern trails.

The Old Salt Trail from Presidio to the great salt lake near Crane crossed at Horsehead. Mexicans with pack mules and their crude wooden-wheeled *carretas* hauled salt from the lake to points throughout northern Mexico.

In 1848, Colonel Jack Hays, the famous Indian fighter, crossed at Horsehead with a party of explorers from San Antonio, seeking a trade route to Chihuahua and back. In March, 1849, Major Robert S. Neighbors, federal Indian agent in Texas, and John S. "Rip" Ford, a veteran of the Mexican War, set out from Austin to mark an emigrant

14

trail as far as Franklin (El Paso). They reached the Horse-head, turned up the Pecos for twenty-eight miles, then struck southwest to Toyah Creek, "a bold stream flowing forty feet wide and eighteen inches deep." Continuing southwest, they camped beside the bubbling waters of Mescalero Springs, at the head of the Toyah, then pivoted around the northern shoulder of the Pah-cut Range (Davis Mountains) and moved westward down a great valley past the terminus of the Apache Mountains and through Guadalupe Pass. Almost before the ink on their report had dried, eager travelers with pack trains and wagons were following their path.

By 1858, the Butterfield Overland Mail, the longest stage-coach route in history, ran from Tipton, Missouri, to California by way of Horsehead. Reaching the Pecos from Mustang Holes and Castle Gap, the coaches turned up the east bank of the river to Pope's Crossing on the New Mexico border, then rocked west below El Capitan Peak, past Crow Springs and Hueco Tanks, and on to Franklin. In August, 1859, the stagecoach company built a station house and scow ferry at Horsehead, and their southern route ran to Fort Stockton, Fort Davis, Deadman's Hole, Van Horn Wells, the Eagle Mountains, and on up the Río Grande. The government paid Butterfield $600,000 a year for his serv-ices, but with the Civil War on the horizon, Congress or-dered the route discontinued. The last stage left the Pecos headed west in mid-March, 1861.

Long before the white man came, the Great Comanche War Trail crossed at Horsehead. For centuries the country was overrun by marauding Comanches and their allies the Kiowas. They ranged from the Texas Panhandle plains to the heart of Mexico. The war trail, laid out skillfully through the mountains and by watering places to the Río Grande, was traveled so regularly in September that the Mexicans began calling the moon of that month the "Bloody Comanche Moon." Chihuahua was a long way from Chapultepec, and her scattered settlements were so poorly defended that it was futile to resist the savage tide that swept even into the distant states of Zacatecas and Durango.

In November and December, the war parties began their return northward with herds of stolen horses, mules, and cattle. Captives were driven with the livestock. The reluctant and the weak were slain and left to rot along the deeply worn trace. Pushing their herds north from the Río Grande, the raiders took no time to graze, and water holes were scarce. When the famished animals reached the Pecos, they would pile into the stream and drink their fill of its brackish water. So many foundered and died bogged down in the quicksand that the crossing became marked with bleaching skulls which gave it its name. Many of the horses and cattle were driven to the main arteries of commerce in the Texas Panhandle and northern New Mexico where they were traded for merchandise—red handkerchiefs and calico. In exchange for their captives, the Indians received guns and ammunition.

Texas suffered so much from Indian depredations that the Rangers were organized to protect its frontier. In 1854, the federal government attempted to confine the Comanches and Kiowas to reservations on the Brazos, but friction continued with the settlers and the effort failed. In 1867, a new reservation was set aside consisting of the Texas Panhandle and all of present Oklahoma west of the Cimarron River and the ninety-eighth meridian. By another treaty two years later, the area was reduced to a tract in southwestern Oklahoma between the North Fork of the Red River and the Washita. The Indians did not stay on this land, however, until after the last outbreak of the Southern Plains tribes in 1874.

By this time, Horsehead Crossing had become an important landmark to early cattle drovers. After the Civil War, Texas found itself with about half of all the cattle in America and no market for them at home. But over in New Mexico, and north in Colorado and Wyoming, were military forts, railroad construction gangs, silver and gold camps, and the reservations of thousands of Indians. In 1866, Charles Goodnight and Oliver Loving drove 3,000 longhorns from Young County to Horsehead and up the Pecos to Fort Sumner, New Mexico. Their trail became known as the Goodnight-Loving Trail, and some 250,000 cattle were driven over this route during the next few years. In 1874 alone, 110,000 head streamed up the east side of the Pecos to northern markets.

A great breeding ground for cattle, with millions of acres of public domain available for free grazing, southeastern New Mexico attracted other widely known Texas cowmen. In 1867, John Chisum moved his herds to Bosque Grande and became the "Cattle King of the Pecos," with more than sixty thousand head wearing his split-ear "jinglebob" mark and "long rail" and "open U" brands. This same year, Oliver Loving died from wounds received in a battle with a Comanche war party.

The long, dry drive from the head of the Middle Concho to Horsehead was a nightmare. Many longhorns perished on the way, and many died when the gaunt survivors of the drive reached the Pecos. The Horsehead allowed an easy approach to water, but before they reached the crossing, many of the thirst-crazed animals jumped from the bluffs into the stream and found themselves stranded under unscalable cliffs. Goodnight lost fifty head at the Pecos on his first trip. Some drovers lost as many as four hundred. Practically every cowman who went up this trail looked on the river and its bleak valley as personal foes. Goodnight called the valley "the graveyard of the cowman's hopes. I hated it! It was as treacherous as the Indians themselves."

Some who drove into the Pecos Valley found sufficient range for their herds and stayed. Couts and Simpson moved their Hashknife cattle from Taylor County across Horsehead in 1879. Colonel W. E. Hughes, of St. Louis, bought Couts's interest in 1880. By fall, Hughes and Simpson were running twenty thousand head on the west side of the Pecos north to the New Mexico line. Twenty miles southeast of Horsehead, on the east bank of the river, J. W. Carter established a ranch in 1879 and enlarged it when the Texas and Pacific Railroad reached the Pecos above Horsehead in 1881.

Early that year, Ranger Charles L. Nevill and some of his men scouted north to the Pecos from their camp near Fort Davis on a tip that Billy the Kid and his gang were in the vicinity and might make trouble for the right-of-way crews. Instead of the Kid, Nevill found "a small town of 200 persons living in tents on the east bank of the river." In August, Ranger S. A. McMurray and some of his men from B Company arrived at "Pecos City" at the request of the railroad to "tone down a rough bunch" who had followed to end-of-track. McMurray found all quiet except for the "drunkenness and rowdyism usually found in a frontier town." The railroad had spanned the river and was pushing west across the alkali flats toward Toyah Springs. "Pecos City" was still a tent town, but it had "moved over about 100 yards west of the river." McMurray further noted: "There is nothing here now except saloons, restaurants and gambling houses."

18

The town grew as a supply point for the river valley. Fort Stockton, to the southeast, freighted most of its goods from Pecos on huge wagons, each pulled by eight oxen driven by Mexican bullwhackers. As lumber arrived from the east, tents were replaced with wooden structures. A hotel, bakery, blacksmith shop, and other businesses sprang up. A wagon bridge was built across the river. Artesian wells were dug to supply the railroad and townsfolk with good water. More cattle outfits arrived, occupying most of present Loving, Ward, and Winkler counties northeast of the river. The largest of these was the "W" ranch, extending thirty miles along the east bank, with thirty thousand head and three hundred saddle horses.

On July 4, 1883, the ranches on both sides of the valley held their first rodeo in Pecos:

Trav Windham won, tied his steer in the middle of Oak Street in 22 seconds flat! Henry Slack's rope broke, no time. Morg Livingston, Fort Stockton, won, Brawley Oates and Ship Parks threw loops too, but it was Trav's day. His proud wife cut one of the blue ribbons off of Bonnie Windham's Sunday dress and they pinned it on Trav. The Hashknives took bigger steps that day and dragged their spurs a little louder than usual in the saloons.

The Pecos women cooked pies and cakes three days in advance, and dinner was served on the grounds to a crowd of five hundred.

The same year, Reeves County was organized and named for Colonel George R. Reeves, a Confederate soldier. A rolling, broken region sloping down from the Guadalupe and Davis mountains on the west and southwest, touching New Mexico, with the Pecos River forming its northeastern boundary, it had been a part of original Bexar Territory,

19

then Santa Fe, claimed under the Treaty of Guadalupe Hidalgo in 1848. It had been a part of Presidio County in 1850, and, in 1852, part of El Paso County, when Presidio was attached to El Paso. It became a part of Tom Green County in 1874, and then Ward County, later carved out of Tom Green. Pecos County was then created, and Reeves County was carved out of Pecos County in 1883.

In November, 1884, Pecos won the county seat election from Toyah. The legality of many of the 253 votes polled was immediately questioned. Legally or not, Pecos won, and the Toyah bunch showed their lack of respect for the official center of Reeves County by riding down and "shooting it up whenever the spirit moved them." J. T. Morris, the first sheriff, served only a brief period. In August, 1885, he was replaced by L. S. Turnbo, who served less than three years. A. D. Irwin took over in April, 1888, and in November, 1890, relinquished the reins to G. A. Frazer. A courthouse and jail had been built and the first bank established in 1891.

By the time Jim Miller arrived in Pecos in August, law and order had begun to take effect. Most of the townspeople had settled down to "making a living, going to church, picnics, engaging in a friendly drink now and then, praying three times a day and fist-fighting twice a week." But it was still a raw land that needed a hard-boiled lawman—someone quick with a gun and not afraid of the devil. The tough element that hung out in "dobie town," the cluster of mud buildings across the railroad tracks, had been about all one officer could handle.

Sheriff Frazer was glad to get some help.

3. The Feud

SHERIFF FRAZER took Miller around town and introduced him to the leading citizens and businessmen. The people were friendly. They shook his hand and wished him luck. Then the sheriff rented a rig and drove him up and down the valley to acquaint him with the ranchers. The ranchers were impressed by Miller's quiet manner and his knowledge of livestock. They nodded approvingly and thought Frazer had picked the right man.

Back in Pecos, Miller took lodging at a hotel across from the bank. He seemed to have a little money and mentioned to Frazer that the hotel business might be a good thing to get into as a side line after he got settled. A new life was opening up to him, and he was determined to make the most of it.

Soon his black coat was seen moving in and out of the bars and gambling dens. The saloonkeepers thought he was too energetic, but they couldn't complain. Miller never visited their places except on official business. He never drank in the saloons, and people noticed he never used tobacco. When the fall religious revivals began in Pecos, he promptly joined church and occupied a seat in the "amen corner" at every service.

Nobody prayed harder than Frazer's deputy. His fervent religious activities endeared him to the good people of the community, and because of his somber coat, black boots and tie, and smooth-crowned black Stetson, they affectionately nicknamed him "Deacon" Jim.

In the fall of 1891, Miller and Sallie Clements were married. Apparently he had kept in touch with her over the years and finally decided he could afford a wife. Mannie Clements came to Pecos with his sister. He liked the town and decided to stay awhile. Jim used him as a deputy when out serving papers and performing his other duties.

Then cattle and horses began disappearing from ranches throughout the valley, and Jim had more work than he could handle.

The ranchers gave Deputy Miller their support. He spent days away from Pecos, alone, trailing the rustlers to the Mexican border but never seeming to catch up with them.

As the situation grew worse, he got himself appointed hide and livestock inspector to give him jurisdiction outside the county. But he was unable, even with this additional authority, to turn up anything of value. In fact, more cattle and horses disappeared than before.

The ranchers became a little more than disturbed. They held a mass meeting in Pecos to discuss ways and means of halting the stealing. One of these ranchers was Barney Riggs, Sheriff Frazer's brother-in-law.

Riggs was a Texan who as a young man had gone to Arizona to work as a ranch foreman. One day he discovered that he and his boss were having an affair with the same woman. Riggs promptly killed his boss and was sentenced to life imprisonment at Yuma.

One morning in late October, 1887, Superintendent Thomas Gates started from the Yuma prison to oversee some men at work, as was his custom. At the sally port he was seized by Librado Puebla and Ricardo Vásquez, both serving thirty years for robbery, and a third convict named López who was doing fifteen years for manslaughter.

Puebla attempted to pinion Gates's arms behind him and at the same time force him outside the walls. Gates struggled fiercely to free himself and shove Puebla to one side to give guard B. F. Hartlee, stationed on the main tower, a chance to shoot. Hartlee was a hardened character, noted for his cool nerve and superb skill with a rifle, but Puebla held a knife at Gates's throat, and Hartlee held his fire.

López and Vásquez ran to the superintendent's house, where the secretary of the prison board, Dick Rule, was working on some papers, and demanded arms. Finding none, they ran to the office, broke open a desk, secured a revolver, and rushed back to assist Puebla. During this interval, Gates had succeeded in partially turning Puebla around. This was Hartlee's chance, and he put a bullet through Puebla's leg. Puebla then drove his knife into Gates's right shoulder, the blade passing between the collarbone and shoulder blade and into his lung.

Secretary Rule had obtained a pistol and followed López and Vásquez from the house. He ran to assist Gates and dealt Puebla a terrific blow over the head, splitting the scalp. Seeing Puebla sink down and thinking he had accomplished his purpose, Rule turned his attention to the others. López, returning to help Puebla, placed his revolver against Gates's head. As he pulled the trigger, Gates, who had freed one hand, knocked the weapon upward and the bullet passed through Puebla's left arm.

López then turned on Rule and at pistol point forced the secretary toward the office. Finally he shot but missed, and Rule shot him through the left side. López fell with his head near the office porch, and Rule, believing he was dead, whirled to meet Vásquez. The same instant, guard Hartlee shot and killed Vásquez.

As Vásquez fell, Rule turned back to the office to get more cartridges. López, lying on his face a few feet away, raised his revolver in both hands and fired at him but missed again, the bullet ripping splinters from the wall at Rule's side.

Meanwhile, Barney Riggs had heard the noise and rushed to the scene. Thinking that it was a fight among the Mexicans and that Gates was trying to separate them, Riggs went to assist Gates and saw the vicious thrust of the knife in the hands of Puebla. Realizing the true nature of the conflict, Riggs ran first to the house and then to the office, but could find no weapon. He was returning empty-handed when he saw López fire at Rule from the ground.

Riggs sprang astride López, wrenched the revolver from his hands, and shot him in the stomach. The next moment he shoved the muzzle of the gun against Puebla's breast. When the hammer fell, Puebla slowly withdrew his bloody knife from Gates's body and turned around. Riggs shot him again, and he sank to the ground. Thus freed, Gates staggered a few paces and collapsed. He was picked up by some onlooking convicts and rushed to the house in a semi-conscious condition.

The affair was over in minutes. Puebla, the most hardened

convict of the lot, lived nearly half an hour. "Well, what do I care. Adios!" he said, and expired.

López died from his belly wound shortly afterward. While still conscious, he untied a handkerchief from his neck and asked that it be sent to his mother.

Superintendent Gates never fully recovered from his wound. He died an invalid.

For his piece of gallantry, Barney Riggs was pardoned. A free man again, he returned to Texas, drifted into Reeves County, and married one of Frazer's sisters.

The ranchers liked Barney despite his macabre boast that he was the only man on record who had killed a man and been sent to prison, then killed two men and got out. He owned a little place near Toyah and generally minded his own business. At the meeting, however, when asked for suggestions, he said:

"First off, I'd get rid of Bud's long-legged deputy. I think he knows who heads up these thieves."

It was a strong accusation, but Miller only laughed. "Maybe Barney's right," he commented. "We ought to think about that."

His church friends gave him their support. And the people began to align themselves in two groups—those who believed in Deacon Jim, and those who did not.

Frazer avoided taking sides. He investigated Miller's record and did not like what he found, but he was a fair-minded man. The mere fact of Miller's kinship with illustrious gun-toters like Mannie Clements, now a resident, and John Wesley Hardin, serving a twenty-five-year sentence for murder in Huntsville prison, proved nothing, he reasoned. Many a man had come to West Texas with a shady past, including Barney Riggs. Pecos was a frontier cowtown where a newcomer made his reputation as he went along, and rehashing dark chapters in his history was considered bad taste. Frazer declined to dismiss his deputy.

A few weeks later, he regretted his tolerance. A Mexican prisoner had to be transferred to Fort Stockton, and Frazer assigned Miller the task. Miller set out with the Mexican, but returned to Pecos far ahead of schedule with a story that for the first time lifted eyebrows.

"The prisoner tried to escape," he said, "and I was forced to kill him."

Frazer received considerable criticism, but the incident soon blew over. Since there was no other witness to the tragedy, Miller's story was accepted.

Barney Riggs gave the sheriff a different version. Refusing to reveal his source of information, he told Frazer: "The Mex knew where Miller disposed of a pair of dun mules south of the border."

Following Barney's directions, Frazer crossed the Río Grande and recovered the animals.

Frazer didn't care what people thought of Miller then; he fired his deputy. He also charged him with theft of the mules, but the case was finally dismissed for lack of evidence.

When election time rolled around in the summer of 1892, Miller ran against Frazer for sheriff. Frazer defeated him easily. A lot of people, however, swore that no man as religious as Deacon Jim could be very bad, and soon Miller was wearing a city marshal's badge.

Miller set up office in the hotel where he stayed. The hotel also became headquarters for his sympathizers and relatives. Mannie Clements became his night officer. Bill Earhart and John Denston, the latter a cousin of Sallie Miller and a gunfighter in his own right, entered the picture, and M. Q.

Hardin of the old DeWitt County clan was frequently seen with the Miller-Clements crowd.

Tension was building up. Still the town remained fairly quiet and a pretty decent place to live.

Then in May, 1893, Frazer had to take some prisoners to Huntsville. The trip took several days, and while he was away, "hell popped loose in Pecos."

The hoodlums took over. Drunks swaggered the streets, the bars and gambling houses ran wide open day and night, and decent citizens were slugged and robbed in back rooms and alleys while Miller strutted about looking smug and smoothing down the front of his black coat. Somebody wired Frazer at Huntsville. In a fighting rage, the sheriff boarded the train for Pecos at once.

Shortly after word got out that the sheriff was on his way home, Hardin was seen in a bar in "dobie town" in quiet conference with a couple of "wild young squirts and trouble-makers," John and Billy Ware. An eavesdropper named Con Gibson heard enough of their conversation to realize they were planning a reception for Frazer when his train pulled in.

"You boys will start a ruckus on the platform," Hardin told the brothers. "Old Bud is already fightin' mad. Naturally he'll try to stop it. That's when a stray bullet will get him."

The Wares were silent for a moment. "And who takes the blame for his killing?" Billy finally spoke up, his voice a little blustery.

"Jim and Mannie has arranged that," Hardin answered. "You just start the fight. And remember—there'll be a different setup for all of us when Jim is sheriff."

Con quickly downed his drink, slid out the back door, and went straight to his brother, James, with the tale.

James Gibson was county clerk and the only county official in town at the time. He almost jumped out of his chair when Con told him what he had overheard.

"Thanks, Con," he said. "I'll send a wire. Let's hope it catches Bud's train before he gets here!"

Gibson's telegram reached Frazer aboard the Southern Pacific. When the sheriff changed trains east of El Paso, he notified Captain John R. Hughes of the Texas Rangers. Hughes and one of his men accompanied Bud to Pecos.

Con Gibson was down at the station with the rest of the town when Frazer stepped off the train with a Ranger on each side of him. The Wares promptly left the platform and disappeared in the crowd. Miller's mouth "flew open a foot," according to one old-timer, "but nothing could faze that man long." He recovered in a second, stepped up, and stuck out his hand. "Glad you're back, Bud—I sure need your help!" he said, and grinned broadly under his sweeping mustache.

Frazer said nothing and refused to shake hands. Con Gibson snickered uneasily, and Miller's face flushed an angry red. Then it was over.

The next day, the Rangers arrested Miller, Clements, and Hardin on a charge of conspiracy to murder Sheriff Frazer and threw them in jail. All except Miller were soon out on bail.

Perhaps it was fear for his life that caused Frazer not to allow Miller out of his sight. He refused all proposals to release his former deputy on bail, thereby arousing the ire of Miller's town friends and some of the leading ranchers.

One of those angered was E. O. Lochausen, who owned a ranch in the valley and operated a hardware store in town. "I'll bet he'll allow the kind of bail I'll offer," Lochausen said, and he rode into Pecos.

It is not clear what bail was offered. The records show that Miller was released, two prominent lawyers from El Paso appeared for his defense, the case concerning Miller and Clements was quashed, and Hardin was indicted as follows:

The State of Texas
vs.   No. 150
M. Q. Hardin

In the and by the authority of the State of Texas:

The Grand Jurors for the County of Reeves, State aforesaid, duly organized as such at the September Term A. D. 1893 of the District Court for said County upon their oaths in said Court, present that M. Q. Hardin on or about the 22nd day of May, 1893, and anterior to the presentment of this Indictment, in the County of Reeves and State of Texas, did then and there unlawfully conspire, combine, confederate, and enter into and make a postive agreement with J. B. Miller and Mannen Clements of and with their malice aforethought to then and there kill and murder G. A. Frazer. Against the peace and dignity of the State.

Witnesses: *John Ware, J. C. Gibson, G. A. Frazer*

G. A. FRAZER, *Sheriff*
GEO. P. LEAKEY, *Deputy Clerk*

Hardin was tried at El Paso on a change of venue and was acquitted. According to the El Paso *Times*, he "got Miller's attorneys to defend him," and Miller and Clements "swore him out of it."

Miller, Clements, and Hardin returned to Pecos. And Bud Frazer checked his weapons more often.

Miller was relieved of his job as city marshal. Many hoped he would leave Reeves County. Instead, he went into the hotel business at Oak and Second streets, where he had lived since coming to Pecos. Mrs. Miller ran the hotel while

29

Jim gambled and generally took things easy. He ignored Frazer for the time being, but the sheriff knew a bee buzzed in his black Stetson. Con Gibson, who had informed on him, knew it too.

Realizing what the results of his previous actions might be, Con took his brother's advice and left the country. He made the mistake of stopping at Eddy, New Mexico. In a saloon there he ran face to face into John Denston.

Con knew why Denston was there and who had put the gunman on his trail, and he did the "most natural thing imaginable." "Damn you, Denston, you've come to kill me!" he blurted, and reached for his gun. As a result, Gibson was buried.

To New Mexico authorities, it was a "plain case of self-defense," and Denston went free.

To Bud Frazer, in Pecos, it was a revenge killing done in cold blood. But he had no chance of pinning anything on Miller. No one would blame Deacon Jim for the acts of his "over-conscientious relatives," and his sizable following in Reeves County still stood by him.

Most of the town was sick of Miller and his hoodlums. Another election was in the offing, and already people were beginning to say it looked like Frazer couldn't do anything about conditions.

The sheriff grew bitter. He no longer feared for his own life. His bitterness burned inside him.

On the morning of April 12, 1894, the frock-coated Miller stepped off his hotel gallery and struck up a conversation with a rancher friend who had just pulled up in a wagon. Miller propped one foot on the hub of a front wheel and was immersed in idle talk about cow business when Frazer walked past on Second Street. Miller's back was toward the sheriff, and he did not notice him.

In a few minutes, Frazer walked past again. Still Miller didn't see him, or if he did, he made no sign. When Frazer turned and started back the third time, the rancher commented, "I wonder why Bud keeps walking by that way."

"Well, I don't know," Miller answered, and turned to stare into the muzzle of the sheriff's six-shooter.

"Jim, you're a thief and a murderer!" Frazer shouted. "Here's one for Con Gibson!"

His six-shooter roared. And the bullet ricocheted right off the front of Miller's black coat!

Startled, Frazer fired again. Miller's hand streaked for his gun, but Frazer's second shot struck him in the right arm near the shoulder, disabling him. The shot undoubtedly saved the sheriff's life.

Miller reached behind himself, whipped out his revolver with his left hand, and blazed away. Shooting left-handed was no specialty of his, however, and his bullet tore the dust at Frazer's feet. Storekeeper Joe Kraus heard the first shot and ran into the street to get a view of the proceedings. Miller's second shot, going wild, caught Joe in the left hip at the waistband. It proved to be only a minor wound, but it convinced the townsman that flying lead was no respecter of persons.

Frazer emptied his six-shooter as fast as he could pull the trigger. He fired three more shots at Miller's black coat, but Miller stayed on his feet and kept coming. Not until Frazer's last bullet struck him below the diaphragm did he drop his revolver and topple over. Then Frazer turned and strode back to his office, unharmed. By all rules of gunfighting, Deacon Jim should have been dead.

His henchmen picked him up from the street and carried him to the hotel. They were amazed to find him very much alive. A quick examination revealed that three of Frazer's bullets had landed within a space of two inches, directly over his heart. They had flattened against a tough steel plate that he wore over his chest concealed by his coat. For the first time, Miller's own men realized why he wore that black coat even in the heat of August.

That evening, when Miller regained consciousness, he grinned up at his friends and said: "Tell Frazer he can't convict me or kill me or run me out of the country. Next time, I'll get *him*!"

4. The Second Battle

DESPITE the protection afforded by the steel breastplate, Miller was a badly wounded man. It would take him months to recover. He was removed to a place twenty miles from town where he could be among friends.

Meanwhile, the feud between him and Frazer threatened to engulf the entire population. Barney Riggs helped Bud line up their relatives and sympathizers; Clements and M. Q. Hardin built a good head of steam for the Miller faction. Many of the leading citizens, including some of the deacons and preachers, voiced themselves passionately in Miller's behalf because they thought he was being persecuted.

Pecos women, however, were concerned about what would happen to their husbands if the feud should break out in a general, shooting war. They appealed to Mrs. Lochausen, the wife of Miller's rancher friend and bondsman. Mrs. Lochausen was a fine, gentle lady, but she had a lot of granite in her character. After Miller's case was quashed and Hardin was acquitted at El Paso, she had cautioned her husband: "You had better quit playing around with that crowd or you'll find yourself in jail with them one of these times." She wasn't afraid of anybody. She got in her buggy and drove out to see Miller.

"Why don't you sell the hotel and leave the country?" she asked him. "There'll be trouble as long as you stay here, and you'll get the rest of us in trouble, too."

"I'm staying," Miller replied. "I'm going to kill Bud Frazer—I'm going to kill him if I have to crawl all the way back to Pecos to do it."

Mrs. Lochausen turned to Miller's wife and asked her the same question. Sallie Miller bristled. "We have as much right to live in this county as anybody. Nobody is going to run us off."

Mrs. Lochausen climbed back into her buggy and left.

There seemed only one other way to prevent a full-scale war from erupting. The county election was in July. Most voters felt that Frazer was a good sheriff, but, hoping to relieve the tension, they put up another candidate, Daniel Murphy. From his bed at the ranch, Miller sided with the new candidate. It was not that Miller was particularly fond of Murphy, but his extra weight was enough to defeat Frazer.

The defeat hurt Bud. His family had been among the first settlers in West Texas. He had been born at Fort Stockton, April 18, 1864. At sixteen, he had joined the Rangers under Captain G. W. Baylor. Later, he had served as deputy sheriff of Pecos County before Reeves was organized from it. His father had been county judge.

Bud put his property up for sale and set out for New Mexico to find a new occupation.

When Miller was able to be up and around, he strode up and down the streets as though he owned Texas, boasting that he had run Frazer out. He made a couple of trips into

New Mexico looking for Frazer, once going as far west as Lordsburg, where he heard Bud was visiting relatives.

One evening, Miller stopped at the Lochausen ranch and asked to borrow "Old Hawk" for the night. Old Hawk was a fast horse, and was always saddled for any kind of emergency. Many people had borrowed him, but this time, remembering the reprimand from his wife, Lochausen hesitated.

"I have to make a short run up the valley and want to be back by morning," Miller told him.

Lochausen let him take the horse.

When Mrs. Lochausen found Miller's horse in the corral and Old Hawk gone, she again took her husband to task. "Why, I'll bet he's on his way somewhere to kill Bud Frazer."

The next day, Lochausen learned that Frazer had been seen at Eddy, making inquiries about a business investment there. The rancher decided he should have been more careful.

Miller rode Old Hawk two days and two nights. When he finally returned from his trip, Mrs. Lochausen looked him straight in the eye, and said: "You were out trying to kill Frazer again, weren't you?"

"That's my business, Mrs. Lochausen," Miller answered, irritation breaking his veneer of politeness.

"No, it isn't. If you had killed Frazer and it come out that you were using our horse, we would have been in a pretty fix."

Miller did his best to placate her. He wanted to keep as many people on his side as possible. It was evident to the Lochausens that he intended to get Frazer even if it meant involving innocent men and women, but they let the matter drop.

In December, 1894, Frazer returned from New Mexico to move his possessions to Eddy, where he was operating a livery business. He had some papers to sign. He stayed with Barney Riggs until Christmas. Barney told Bud that Miller had been boasting he would kill him. On December 26, Frazer rode into Pecos to settle the last of his affairs.

He left his horse in a feed yard off Second Street and started down to the bank. In front of Zimmer's blacksmith shop he met Deacon Jim. In a flash he recalled Barney's warning, and he didn't wait to see what Miller would do. He drew his six-shooter and began firing.

His first shot caught Miller in the right arm. His second bullet tore into Miller's left leg. Then he aimed at Miller's heart and pulled the trigger again.

And Deacon Jim, disabled as he was, stood there, gun out and throwing lead left-handed.

After another shot at the man's heart, Frazer became confused. He still didn't know about that steel breastplate. He knew his aim was true, and he was a brave man, but this business spooked him. Suddenly, he turned and fled.

Again Miller's henchmen carried him from the street. They wanted to go after Frazer, but Miller refused the offer. He thought it best to further his cause in town by trying the legal way first. He swore to a charge of assault with intent to murder, and Daniel Murphy, the new sheriff, arrested Bud.

A Reeves County grand jury indicted Frazer on March 4, 1895. District Judge Buckler decided that Frazer could not receive an impartial trial in Reeves and ordered the case transferred to El Paso County.

The trial was set for the second week in April. By this time, John Wesley Hardin had been released from Huntsville. Wes had studied law in prison and had been admitted to the bar in Gonzales County, where he had gone to look after his children. His wife had died before he received his pardon. He had practiced law nearly a year and had begun work on his autobiography when he became embroiled once more in Gonzales politics and factional warfare. Naturally belligerent and too full of strong convictions to keep to the middle of the road, he backed a candidate for sheriff in a bitter contest in which bloodshed was narrowly averted. His man lost the election, and Hardin left Gonzales. He had drifted to San Antonio, then to Junction, in Kimble County. In the nearby town of London, he met and wed a young lady who left him a few days afterward. He never saw her again. He was casting about for a new place to hang up his shingle and continue his writing when he received word of the small war involving his relatives in Reeves County. Since Hardin was a cousin of Sallie's father and was known for his abilities in former years, Jim Miller thought it a good idea to retain him as special attorney to aid in the prosecution of Bud Frazer.

To Wes it was a clan call, or at least an echo of the fury of his old cowboy and feuding days. With thirty or more notches on his six-shooters and generally regarded as the most dangerous gunfighter in the blood-soaked history of the border country, he took the road west toward Horsehead Crossing. He rode leisurely. In every town he visited, people wanted to see him. And Wes was graciously accommodating. He did not reach Pecos until late in March.

Like the other towns, Pecos greeted him as if he were royalty, to the great satisfaction of the Miller-Clements crowd. One ranch threw a big party which Miller and Hardin attended, consuming a quantity of homemade ice cream— a rarity on this part of the frontier. Hardin was as handsome and gentle in his manner as Deacon Jim. In the words of one authority, "probably never before had so much ruthlessness and so much refinement been seen together."

Hardin spent a week with Miller, making acquaintances and plotting their case. As the date of the trial approached, half the population of Reeves County went to El Paso. Wes went with Mannie Clements and M. Q. Hardin, both armed with Winchesters.

Jeff Milton, El Paso's famous chief of police, got wind of their coming. He had five semiautomatic shotguns with folding handles planted in convenient places. When he heard that Wes and his two confederates had arrived in town and were making the rounds carrying six-shooters and rifles, he went looking for them. Six-shooters were expected, if prohibited, but the rifles were another matter. He located the trio in McClain's saloon.

Although Milton had never seen Hardin, he recognized the gunfighter by his bearing. He walked directly up to him and said: "I do not allow six-shooters to be worn on the streets of this city. You will have to leave them and your rifles with the bartender."

Hardin looked him over, his narrow, gray eyes cold and calculating. "Do you know who you are talking to?" he asked.

"I think I do," Milton replied. "And I think you and your friends know it would be smart to put away your guns now before somebody takes a notion to start something."

Milton's quiet, businesslike manner gave Hardin pause. After a moment, he said, "All right, Chief, we'll abide by your law."

"That's all I ask," said Milton, and he left the saloon.

Hardin gave him no trouble, and the El Paso *Times*

Jim Miller as he appeared at Pecos, Texas, in the 1890's.

Emanuel "Mannen" Clements, Sr., rancher in McCulloch and Runnels counties, Texas, and brother of Jim, Gip, and Joe Clements, cousins of the notorious John Wesley Hardin. Jim Miller married Emanuel Clements' daughter, Sallie. Clements was killed at Ballinger, Texas, on March 29, 1887.

Joe Clements (left) and John Gipson "Gip" Clements of the famous Taylor-Sutton feud, brothers of Emanuel Clements, Sr., and cousins of John Wesley Hardin.

Sheriff G. A. "Bud" Frazer with a group of friends and relatives at Pecos, Texas, in the 1890's. Standing, l. to r.: Sheriff Frazer, Tom White, G. M. Frazer, Allen Heard, John Rooney, Tom Babb. Seated, l. to r.: Lee Heard, Herman Koehler, Charles Buster.

Courtesy Bill Leftwich, Pecos, Texas

A gambling scene in a Pecos, Texas, saloon in the 1890's. The man with the white hat seated at the table is believed to be Jim Miller.

Courtesy Division of Manuscripts,
University of Oklahoma Libraries

Emanuel "Mannie" Clements, Jr., the good friend and brother-in-law of Jim Miller, served as deputy and city policeman under Miller at Pecos. Here he is shown while serving as constable at El Paso, where he was killed in Tom Powers' Coney Island Saloon on December 29, 1908.

Courtesy Division of Manuscripts,
University of Oklahoma Libraries

Texas Ranger Captain John R. Hughes, who accompanied Sheriff Bud Frazer to Pecos when Frazer received a telegram warning him that he had been marked for ambush.

Jeff Milton, chief of police at El Paso at the time of Frazer's trial. He made John Wesley Hardin and his party put away their six-shooters and rifles.

noted: "It is understood that the people interested in the Frazer-Miller case from Pecos [who] came to El Paso armed to the teeth [have been] taught the lesson that El Paso has her own peace officers. The day for man-killers in this town has passed. . . ."

The trial finally got under way. Because of conflicting testimony, the jurors could not agree. Judge Buckler discharged the jury on April 14. Frazer's lawyers asked for another change of venue, and a second trial was set at Colorado City, in Mitchell County, for May, 1896. Most of the legal aides and bodyguards left town the next day. Frazer returned to his livery business at Eddy, and Miller went back to Pecos.

Deacon Jim was disgusted. To make matters worse, his lawyer decided to stay in El Paso. Wes Hardin rented a room and re-established his law practice. He also tried to wind up the work on his book. But the border city was so infested with undesirables and so alive with intrigue and conflict that he found its saloons and card rooms more interesting. He drank and gambled and became involved in an unpleasant scandal or two. His law business fell off. Finally he quarreled with Constable John Selman, slayer of many notorious desperadoes, over the arrest of one of his clients by the constable's son, John Selman, Jr., who was a city policeman. On August 19, Wes was standing at the bar in the Acme Saloon when the elder Selman entered. Selman must have seen Hardin's first quick movement in the back bar mirror, for he whipped out his pistol and put a bullet through the gunfighter's head.

As a result, Hardin was unable to do anything for Deacon Jim at Colorado City. He couldn't have helped much, anyway. The Mitchell County jurors, who didn't know Miller

5. Double-barreled Death

FOR the next three months, Miller and Frazer, through a system of spies and friends in Pecos and Eddy, kept tab on each other's movements. In September, Bud came to Toyah to visit his mother and sister and pay a political debt by aiding a friend who was running for office.

Frazer knew that Miller was aware of his presence in Reeves County, but he wasn't worried. On his right hip, in quick reach, he carried a specially built revolver. Barney Riggs had to make a business trip to Fort Stockton, and before he left, Bud explained the gun's operation: "The sights are set to kill a man half a mile away, and it's loaded with 'explosion balls' that will blow a hole in a man twice the size of an ordinary bullet."

"Be careful," Barney warned. "Miller may never give you a chance to use it."

Barney proved to be right. On the night of September 13, Bill Earhart met Miller at the outskirts of Pecos with two horses. Miller had walked out of town. Frazer's friends would have spotted him had he ridden out. The two men galloped to Toyah and slipped into a front room Earhart had reserved at the hotel. The hotel was directly across the street from the saloon where Frazer spent much of his time every morning.

Miller arose early. He sent Earhart down to the saloon while he watched from the hotel window.

At nine o'clock, Frazer entered the saloon as usual. Earhart was playing seven-up with Johnson Tate, Andy Cole, and J. E. Jerrell. They had just finished a game when Frazer came in, and Earhart gave the former sheriff his seat at the table. Frazer knew Earhart was a Miller sympathizer, but Earhart appeared to have severed relations with the Pecos crowd. For several months he had been living at La Luz, New Mexico, in Doña Ana County. Bud must have wondered what he was doing in Toyah, but when Earhart pulled up another chair and joined the group as a spectator, he aroused no suspicion. Pat Flowers was tending bar on the east side of the room. J. D. Shelton, another Toyah citizen, stood beside Cole with his back to the door, watching the game. The stage was set for the last act of the tragedy.

It is alleged that Earhart signaled Miller, but just how he did it was never determined. Miller came down from the room and left the hotel by a side door, carrying a double-barreled shotgun. He glanced up and down the street, then walked rapidly across to the saloon.

Frazer was facing the door but somehow failed to see the twin muzzles that nosed through the opening aimed at his Adam's apple. None of the men in the room saw the weapon. All they heard was a roar. The double charge practically blew Frazer's head from his body. The next moment, the room was empty, and all that was left of Frazer sat limp in the chair.

42

"All of a sudden the room exploded like dynamite had hit the floor," one of the witnesses said afterward. "I happened to be looking at Bud, and like to have fainted when I saw his whole head disappear in a clot of splashing blood and bone. That's all I took time to see. I dived through the window, taking glass and all with me. Next thing I remember I was under my bed three blocks away, shivering like hell."

Andy Cole was more specific:

We were in the front part of the saloon. The building sets near north and south . . . two rooms divided by a partition with an opening [into the back room] but no door to it. Main entrance north. We were in the north part. . . . Mr. Tate was sitting on my left. Mr. Jerrell was on my right. Bud Frazer was sitting opposite me. The distance from the front door to the table is about twelve feet. The door was partly open when I sat down to play. . . . The sound of the gun first drew my attention to the door and to Miller. There were two shots fired, only a second elapsed between them. I looked up as soon as the gun fired, but did not see Miller until after the second shot on account of smoke and dust. I did not recognize him when I first saw him. He had on a different hat from what he usually wore. . . . He was standing just inside the north door with gun in hand and just broke it to throw the shells out. I did not look at Frazer. I was getting outdoors and looking at the man who had the gun. I went to the depot. . . . I went back to the saloon in about an hour. I could see where shot struck the partition. They looked like buckshot.

Johnson Tate added one pertinent point to the story:

I was sitting next to the bar, Cole on my right, Jerrell in front of me. Frazer was sitting to my left. A shot broke up the game. Two shots were fired. . . . *The door was partly closed so the players could not be seen from the outside; when the door opened, the light that came in caused me to*

43

look around [author's italics]. I looked over my right shoulder. The first thing I saw was a gun in the hands of Mr. Miller who was inside the door. The muzzle of the gun was about three feet away and pointed toward me. I turned [from] my chair and ran outside.

Earhart denied that Frazer had been slain in cold blood:

Bud had his cards in his left hand. I suppose he saw Miller [when the door opened and the light came in], as he threw up his head and dropped his right hand to his side in a quick reach. The first shot was then fired. Bud had a new gun. He never told me why he carried it, but I had my own ideas, knowing of the previous difficulty he had with Miller.

As soon as the word reached Frazer's sister, she came running into the saloon and threw herself across his body, sobbing. She searched the body for his revolver, but someone had already removed it. She asked Pat Flowers to lend her a gun, but Flowers refused. She returned home, armed herself with a pistol, and, accompanied by her mother, set out for Pecos.

After the killing, Miller walked to the hotel, got his horse, and rode back to Pecos. Frazer's mother and sister arrived almost as soon as he did. They "confronted him in great grief and anger." The sister covered him with her pistol.

Miller told her, "If you try to use that gun, I'll give you what your brother got—I'll shoot you right in the face!"

The girl lowered the weapon, but she gave Miller a tongue lashing that neither he nor the bystanders ever forgot. Miller then ordered all the Frazer clan to leave Reeves County, and added, "That includes Barney Riggs." The two women retreated.

An inquest was held that afternoon, and Sheriff Murphy

filed an affidavit for a warrant before Justice of the Peace P. H. Merriman:

In the name and by the authority of the State of Texas, I, Daniel Murphy, do solemnly swear that I have good reason to believe and do believe that J. B. Miller, on or about the 14th day of September A. D. 1896, and before the making and filing of this complaint in the County of Reeves and state aforesaid—did then and there unlawfully with and of his malice aforethought kill and murder G. A. Frazer by shooting him the said G. A. Frazer with a gun. Against the peace and dignity of the State.

Murphy put Miller in jail, and Deacon Jim sent for his lawyers in El Paso.

Frazer's mother and sister returned to Toyah. Barney Riggs had returned from his trip to Fort Stockton. He had already learned the details of Bud's death, how Miller had spent the night in Earhart's hotel room, and what Earhart had testified at the inquest. When his wife told him of Miller's threats, Barney shoved a .45 Colt into the waistband of his pants, saddled a fresh horse, and rode to Pecos.

He didn't see Miller. Miller was still in jail. But he found Earhart, with John Denston, at the bar in the Orient Saloon.

"I hear your roommate said for me to leave the country," Barney drawled.

Suddenly he was looking into the muzzle of Earhart's revolver. "You should have left," growled the gunman, and his six-shooter roared. Barney ducked enough that the bullet only grazed him. He came up with his .45 in his hand, returning the fire.

His first bullet caught Earhart between the eyes. He died instantly. Denston tried to grab Barney's revolver, but "got scared and fled through the door." Barney sprang after him.

As Denston ran west up the street, Barney fired again. His second shot tore off the back of Denston's head.

A crowd gathered around the body in the roadway. Mark Mitchell, a close friend of Con Gibson, whom Denston had killed at Eddy, leaned over and scooped some of his brains from the dust.

"What you going to do with them, Mark?" Barney asked.

Mitchell grinned. "Send them to Con's widow at Comfort, Texas."

Barney laughed and shoved his .45 back in his trousers. He surrendered to Sheriff Murphy and posted bond to await action of the grand jury. "I'm going home now," he said. "Miller claims the county is too small for the two of us. I agree. Tell him that I'm going to have to kill him!"

Miller got the message. He was indicted for the murder of Frazer and was granted a change of venue to Eastland County. As soon as he was out on bail, he held a conference with his cronies. They advised him that a change of scenery might be good for his health. Even Mannie Clements admitted that a metal breastplate was no protection against a man like Riggs. He aimed at men's heads!

Riggs was indicted for the murder of Denston and Earhart. He got a change of venue to El Paso and was acquitted May 18, 1897. "A clear case of self-defense," said the El Paso *Times*, "Earhart drew first. The jury which brought in the verdict of 'not guilty' was out only long enough to write the two words down."

Riggs returned to Toyah. But long before that, Jim Miller decided he had had enough of turbulent Reeves County.

6. Gun for Hire

WITH his trial coming up at Eastland, Deacon Jim moved there early in December, 1896. Eastland was a frontier town of less than one thousand population on the Texas and Pacific Railroad not far from Fort Worth. Eastland County had been created in 1858 from Bosque, Travis, and Coryell; organized in 1873, it was named for Captain W. M. Eastland, a Texas patriot who took part in the Battle of Mier. Generally rolling to hilly in the west, broken by valleys in the east, and drained by the North and South Leon rivers, it was largely an agricultural and livestock district, far enough from West Texas, Miller's lawyers figured, that "a jury fair and impartial" could be had and "no state of public opinion" existed. It was Deacon Jim's idea to move to Eastland well in advance of his trial.

Being a quiet, temperate man, he had no trouble getting acquainted. He brought letters of introduction from Pecos friends, had his church membership transferred, and contributed generously to local charities. He even took a job

47

managing a local hotel. In addition, he was a family man now—he had a boy five years old and another nearly two. By the time his case was called in June, 1897, he had succeeded in impressing the town's best citizens.

His trial was hard fought and lasted nearly three weeks. People came from all over Texas to witness the proceedings. More than 150 people came from West Texas alone. According to the Fort Worth *Register*, at least half of these consisted of "all the badmen between the Pecos river and El Paso," and it was rumored that one hundred Winchester rifles were being shipped in by train. This caused a great deal of excitement. Special deputy sheriffs and Texas Rangers were called in to assist the local authorities. But nothing happened. Miller scoffed at the affair as nothing more than an effort on the part of the prosecution to prejudice him in the eyes of the good citizens of Eastland.

His Pecos friends swore he was a peaceable man, and one church deacon testified that Jim's conduct was as "exemplary as that of a minister of the gospel." Miller called for Denton Robertson, John Brooks, J. B. Prewit, H. C. Zimmer, Joe Kraus, Johnson Tate, and Pat Flowers of Reeves County; Tom Morrison of Mitchell; Tod Callahan of Midland; Jack Coger of Howard; and H. S. Ripkin and George Scarborough of El Paso as witnesses material to his defense. Robertson, Morrison, Callahan, Brooks, Coger, Ripkin, and Scarborough testified to various conversations they had had with the deceased G. A. Frazer in which Frazer had threatened the life of the defendant. Prewit, Zimmer, and Kraus testified to former assaults made upon the defendant by the deceased. Earhart's deposition, taken at the inquest, was admitted, and Johnson Tate and Pat Flowers, refuting the testimony of Cole, Jerrell, and Shelton, declared that Miller had acted in self-defense.

Despite this "high sounding rigamarole," eleven jurors voted to convict Deacon Jim. For some reason, one juror held out. Evidently, gambler that he was, Miller held an ace up his sleeve in case everything else failed.

During the next few months, he traveled all over Eastland County with the minister of his church, holding prayer meetings. At his second trial in January, 1899, he was acquitted on the ground that "he had done no worse than Frazer."

After his acquittal, Miller reverted to his old tactics. According to one story, he bought half-interest in a local saloon, on credit, then pretended to leave town. During his absence, his partner and Sallie Miller were seen riding together in a buggy, although their relations seem to have been proper. While they were in the buggy, however, an accomplice of Miller reported to the partner that Miller was out to kill him. The partner left town without packing his suitcase and was never heard from again. Deacon Jim took over the saloon, then sold it and moved to Hall County.

Memphis, seat of this land of rolling prairies and low mesas along the Prairie Dog Town Fork of the Red River, was located on the Colorado and Southern Railroad from Fort Worth to Denver and was a major shipping point for cattlemen in this part of northwestern Texas and the old Greer County section of Oklahoma Territory. Miller bought a saloon in Memphis and reportedly got himself appointed a Texas Ranger.

The records do not show that he was ever a member of this picturesque fighting corps of manhunters, but there is some evidence that he worked part time as a deputy sheriff. In this capacity, he became involved in a murder investigation in adjoining Collingsworth County.

A man named Joe Beasley was accused of blowing the head off a prominent citizen with a shotgun, Miller's favorite weapon. Beasley denied the charge, and there was considerable doubt that he had pulled the trigger. But Miller turned up an old friend from his Coryell County days, Joe Earp, who claimed to have witnessed the murder and identified Beasley as the killer. A reward of ten thousand dollars had been offered for the arrest and conviction of the slayer. Beasley was indicted and granted a change of venue to Vernon, in Wilbarger County.

A few days before the trial, Dee Harkey happened to be on a train trip to Eastland. He was playing cards with three strangers and dropped the remark that he had served as a special deputy during Miller's trial there. One of the men became immediately interested.

"Do you know Joe Earp?" he asked.

Harkey told him he did. "I met him in Eastland. He was at the trial."

The stranger wanted to know if Earp had gone back to Coryell County. Harkey didn't think so. "I saw him in Eastland less than a month ago. We played cards together."

The stranger asked if Dee had seen Earp on a certain date. Harkey thought back, and nodded. "That was on a Sunday—the night we played cards."

The stranger then introduced himself as Joe Beasley's lawyer and told Harkey that Earp claimed to have seen his client kill a man in faraway Collingsworth County that same night. Harkey agreed to go to Vernon and testify.

Somehow, Joe Earp learned of his coming. When Harkey got off the train at Vernon, Earp greeted him and introduced him to another man who he claimed was the district attorney. This surprised Harkey, who "wasn't sure the man was the district prosecutor." When Earp asked Harkey to go with them to the hotel where they could talk, Harkey replied: "I'll do my talking on the street, not in a hotel room where

I might be killed." Later, District Attorney Stanley of the Forty-sixth Texas Judicial District came around, and Harkey accompanied him to the hotel, where Earp turned state's evidence, admitting that Beasley was innocent and that Miller had "fixed this frame" to collect the ten thousand dollars.

Beasley's case was dismissed, and Miller was indicted for subornation of perjury. District Attorney Stanley prosecuted the case vigorously. Miller was convicted and sentenced to two years in the penitentiary. But again, Deacon Jim's dark angel seemed to be guiding his destiny. His lawyer took the case to the Texas Court of Appeals and won a reversal on a faulty indictment.

Miller remained in jail until the case was reversed. When the charge was dismissed, he boarded the train for Memphis. Judge Charles R. Brice of Hall County and some of his brothers were on the train, and Miller told them: "Joe Earp turned state's evidence on me, and no man can do that and live. Watch the papers, boys, and you'll see where Joe Earp died." Three weeks later, Earp was shot from ambush in Coryell County.

Miller was never arrested for this crime, though he boasted to Judge Brice, "I rode a hundred miles that night and sent a telegram to establish an alibi."

The judge never mentioned this statement until years afterward. He knew Jim Miller and knew his life wouldn't have been worth a "plugged peso" if he had spoken out. He was further discouraged by the mysterious death of District Attorney Stanley.

Soon after Miller's release, Stanley had come to Memphis on business and had stayed at the local hotel. He had become sick the night he arrived and died the next morning. The doctor who examined him gave peritonitis as the cause of his death, and the incident was forgotten. Later, the doctor told one of Judge Brice's brothers that Stanley had died of arsenic poisoning. The doctor also said that upon further investigation he had discovered that the regular hotel cook had not been on duty the night the district attorney became ill. A new cook, a friend of Miller's, had replaced him. The day Stanley died, the new cook disappeared. The doctor did not report the incident "because he feared Deacon Jim."

Miller soon left Memphis. Some authorities claim he moved down the Red River to Gainesville, in Cooke County, where he had an appointment as a deputy United States marshal. Again, there is no record that he ever served as a federal officer. Whatever his business in Cooke County, his stay was of short duration. In 1900, he settled in Fort Worth.

He rented a rambling mansion opposite the courthouse on Weatherford Street, and Mrs. Miller turned it into a rooming establishment. Jim joined church and otherwise made himself a familiar figure around town. The Delaware Hotel (built on the site of the lavish and gas-lighted El Paso Hotel opened by C. K. Fairfax in 1878) was known to prominent cattlemen whose herds grazed in West Texas and the Indian Territory above Red River. It was also a popular meeting place for local business and professional people. Almost any evening Miller could be seen occupying an armchair among the loungers.

Ostensibly, he dabbled in real estate and gambled for a living; secretly, he had evolved into a deadly, emotionless machine. The worm that had lain concealed in him for so long had gnawed to the surface.

The word went out that his gun was for hire. He would kill anyone for a price.

7. Sheepmen and Nesters

MORE and more sheepmen were encroaching on the big ranches in West Texas. The sheep business was not new to the cattlemen. The padres in the missions had sheep, and the first Spanish ranchers between San Antonio and the Río Grande had raised sheep and cattle together. The colonists who came from the United States with Stephen F. Austin brought sheep with them. After the Mexican War, they pushed their herds into the hills west of Austin. At the outbreak of the Civil War, sheep were scattered throughout the timbered region bordering the plains. Here they remained until the Plains Indians were suppressed and the cattlemen moved their longhorn herds westward over the millions of acres of free grass.

Following the Civil War and the attendant boom in the wool market, sheep raising, as well as cattle raising, experienced sudden growth. In 1866, nearly two million dollars' worth of wool was shipped from Galveston. By 1870, the timbered canyons along the Nueces, Sabinal, Medina,

Guadalupe, and Llano rivers had become one of the largest wool-producing areas in the world. Then someone discovered that the hill country north of San Antonio was better for sheep. It was higher and drier; foot rot was unheard of and scab seldom known. In the next two decades the industry spread north and west onto the plains.

A high-powered advertising campaign conducted by those who wanted to develop western Texas was largely responsible for this postwar expansion. Newspapers, magazines, and handbills distributed by half a dozen big land companies painted glowing pictures of the plains and its opportunities. The Texas legislature created a State Board of Immigration, with agencies as far away as Europe, and the railroads devoted efforts to the same purpose. The potentialities of sheep raising were especially set forth. All a man needed was "a few ewes, a bag of beans, a sack of flour, and a plug of chewing tobacco." No winter shelter or feeding was necessary. Within a year he could sell his wool and mutton, keep his ewes to increase his herd, and, within five years, become a millionaire. Sheepmen from the Middle West, the eastern states, and across the seas came to Texas by the hundreds.

Sheep raisers necessarily had to be outsiders. No self-respecting Texan could bear the stigma of the name "sheepherder," regardless of the profits to be made. The range belonged to the longhorn, said the cattlemen, because they were on it first. Woollies smelled, trampled out the grass, and cut up the sod with their cloven hoofs, leaving nothing for other animals. To the cowboy, who gauged a man by the way he sat a horse, anything that had to be tended on foot was unworthy of a "white" man's consideration. Running sheep was entirely an occupation for foreigners and Mexicans. Call a Texan a liar or a thief, and you might ride off unscathed; call him "sheepherder," and you were bound to receive a bullet from his six-shooter or rifle.

The war between sheepmen and cattlemen broke out in the 1870's and reached its climax in the 1880's. With the range closing in and free grass becoming less plentiful, the war was renewed soon after 1900. Each faction claimed certain areas by right of being there first. They set up dead lines, and the fellow who crossed them took the consequences.

Sheepmen paid little attention to trespassing cows. A cow either left a range that had been "sheeped off" or starved. If she was shot accidentally, the herder had beef to eat and hide to mend his shoes. He never let the cow's owner find out. Neither did he feel badly about it; it was all part of protecting his range.

The ethical sheepman never moved through another man's range without obtaining permission. But West Texas had its share of "drifters" who grazed their sheep anywhere. They were liars and thieves and were treated as such. With the Alamo still a vivid memory in the Anglo-Texan heart, the feeling against Mexicans was strong. Lax supervision on the frontier required that frontiersmen make their own laws. There didn't seem to be a law against killing Mexicans—and sheepherders. Cattlemen considered killing sheepmen as legitimate as shooting stock thieves. In many instances, sheep were shot and killed or wounded, or wild horse herds were stampeded into flocks, crippling and scattering them in every direction.

A few big sheep raisers who could afford the expense hired Mexican gunmen from below the Río Grande and fought back. But for the most part, the sheepman's defense was diplomacy or strategy. He was usually outnumbered, sometimes unarmed, and often on foot. In such cases, more cuss words and threats were exchanged than lead.

A number of sheepmen were able to obtain limited range by leasing or buying it. Using the threat that the state might take a hand and send in the Rangers, they were able to call cowmen's bluffs and stand on their rights. In such cases, cattlemen found it necessary to hire a professional to do their work—a man like Jim Miller.

For the next few years, Deacon Jim rode in and out of Fort Worth. He often would be gone for weeks at a time. His standard price for killing sheepherders was $150 a head, and he was reported to have murdered a dozen of them.

The records show he killed two men in Midland County. In the summer of 1902, he killed two more in Ward County near the Pecos River. There were three men in this party. Miller claimed that he had come upon them while they were herding stolen cattle and that they had opened fire on him. Two died with bullets from his Winchester in their brains. The third, seriously wounded, clung to his horse, escaped, and was never apprehended.

Later, Miller shot two Mexicans whom he caught butchering a steer from a herd he was guarding near the New Mexico line.

During one of his sojourns in Fort Worth, Miller boasted to an acquaintance, with evident pride: "I have killed eleven men that I know about; I have lost my notch stick on sheepherders I've killed out on the border."

While cattlemen had a genuine disrespect for sheepmen, they developed a bitter hatred for another type of individual who even more seriously affected the economic status of the range during these years—the dry farmer.

His attempts at agriculture without irrigation, in a region

that lacked sufficient rainfall already, were more ruinous to the grazing areas of the West than sheep, according to the stockmen. The homesteader "raised nothing but kids and cries for help," and cattlemen and sheepmen alike had to fight to keep the grass from being plowed under.

This was the ugliest phase of the range war. Fences were cut, farmers' fields were trampled by livestock, and much red blood was spilled. Stockmen fenced their own ranges to keep the homesteaders out, and this brought on an argument between the "free-grass" and "fenced-range" men. They cut each other's fences as well as farmers'. But generally they teamed up, and cattle and sheep were thrown closer together as both factions struggled for their very existence.

In the big ranch country in the Texas Panhandle, there was an "open season on nesters." By now, Deacon Jim's reputation was well established. His price for nesters was the same as for sheepherders.

A fight was brewing between cattlemen and nesters who were cutting in on the ranges around Lubbock. Representing the farmers was James Jarrott, a young lawyer with a good education and plenty of nerve. When the ranchers attempted to move him off his homestead, he took them to court and won his case on a technicality. Then he took the side of the farmers and began winning lawsuits in their favor as fast as the cattlemen's lawyers filed them.

First Mrs. Jarrott received a note which read: "You will take your children and leave the country. You will never hold that piece of land." Her husband took the note to the district attorney and demanded an investigation. Nothing came of it.

Jarrott received other warnings. He ignored them and continued to win lawsuits. He was getting in the hair of the range barons.

One day, a stranger wearing a black coat, and armed with a Winchester saddle gun and an ivory-handled six-shooter appeared on the streets of Lubbock. He rode on the next day and was forgotten.

A few nights later, James Jarrott started home in his buggy. He stopped to water his team at a windmill near his farm. As he stepped down to unhook the traces, a rifle cracked from a clump of weeds nearby. Jarrott clutched his chest and sank to the ground.

As he writhed in the dust, the rifle cracked again. He gasped and struggled up on his hands and knees. A shadowy figure rose from the weeds and levered another cartridge into his Winchester. He walked close to his victim and fired a third time.

The bullet ripped into Jarrott's neck and shoulder. He sank back to the ground. But he was still alive, and a fourth shot was required to finish him.

By Miller's own account to an acquaintance, "He was the hardest damned man to kill I ever tackled."

Miller told the same person that he received five hundred dollars for the murder of lawyer Jarrott.

He never said what his total take was from the sheep and nester wars, but it was obvious he had done pretty well for himself. He replaced his old smooth-crowned black hat with a fine white Stetson and bought himself a new, finely tailored black coat. He sported a diamond ring and wore an expensive diamond stud in his shirt front.

With his modest manners and good looks, he was the very essence of a successful businessman. But his business was killing for money. He had no more scruples about taking human life than he had about killing coyotes. He was a frontier enigma in that he could stand up and shoot it out in a face-to-face encounter or murder a man from the darkness with a shotgun or rifle.

He no longer tried to hide his nature under the cloak of politeness. He discussed his crimes with friends and seemed to take special pleasure in telling about the worst things he had done. He was careful, however, not to relate them in such a manner that they could be proved later. And he made no bones of letting his listeners know that betrayal meant death.

Miller spent most of the winter of 1904 and the spring of 1905 in Fort Worth, speculating in real estate and pulling any shady deal that turned up. Once he defrauded a Portales, New Mexico, man out of one thousand sheep by paying him with a worthless check. The sheepman did nothing. He thought it better to lose his money than his life.

Miller was also credited with shipping some stolen mules to Carl Adamson at Alamogordo. Adamson was related to Miller and Mannie Clements by marriage. He was indicted for possessing stolen livestock, but the case was finally dismissed.

Miller's prize scheme was a real estate promotion which involved another Fort Worth man named Frank Fore.

Fore dealt mainly in city lots. Miller had several that looked beautiful on a map but actually were in the Gulf of Mexico, and Fore sold them sight unseen to trusting buyers. When Fore realized where the lots were located, he became alarmed and threatened to go before the grand jury.

Miller detested grand juries. One morning during a cattle-men's convention at the Delaware Hotel, he cornered Fore in a washroom just off the lobby, drew a revolver from the side pocket of his trousers, and killed him with a single shot.

As a crowd gathered, Jim bent over his former partner,

and tears rolled down his cheeks. "It's awful," he wailed, "to have to kill a friend—I did everything I could to keep him from reaching for his gun!" Then he dried his eyes, walked up the street, and surrendered to the sheriff.

Tom Coggin and Jenks Clark, of San Saba County, signed as sureties on his appearance bond. At Miller's trial in April, 1905, the two cattlemen testified that they were in the lavatory when the killing occurred and that the shooting was in self-defense. The district attorney attempted to show that these "eye-witnesses" were in the lobby and that Fore was in the washroom alone, but the testimony favored Deacon Jim. He was acquitted.

Afterward, a friend asked him, "How did old Frank take it?"

Miller grinned. "When he saw my gun, he squawked like a Dominecker rooster!"

8. Buckshot for a Marshal

JIM Miller's next publicized killing occurred in 1906 north of the Red River in the Chickasaw Nation, Indian Territory. This was the year before Oklahoma statehood, and change was in the air.

Indian Territory encompassed the seven small tribes of the Quapaw Agency and the nations of the Five Civilized Tribes—Cherokees, Creeks, Seminoles, Chickasaws, and Choctaws. It was not a governmental unit like Oklahoma Territory, which generally covered the western half of the future state. Oklahoma Territory had a governor, secretary of state, supreme court judges appointed by the President of the United States, a legislature elected by popular vote, and county governments, the officials of which were elected by the people. In Indian Territory, each nation had its system of district and national officials and courts for the benefit of its citizens. Tribal laws were enforced by district sheriffs, elected by the Indians, and by Lighthorsemen appointed by the principal chief. Lighthorsemen were subject to duty anywhere in the nation as the principal chief directed. Non-citizens, who were mostly white, had no voice in the selection of Indian officials governing them, no legislature, no form of county government, and no vote in presidential elections. They were governed by federal laws and the laws of Arkansas, administered by federal courts and enforced by United States marshals, their deputies, and Indian Police appointed by the secretary of the interior.

Congress had extended the jurisdiction of the federal courts of Arkansas over the Indian Territory in 1834. In 1844, a federal court was established at Fort Smith and, until 1889, people having business there had to travel as far as three hundred miles from the western reaches of the Chickasaw Nation. Before the railroads were completed in the 1880's, these trips were made by horseback, buggy, and wagon.

In 1889, Congress established the first white man's court at Muskogee. While principally a court of civil jurisdiction, it was given exclusive, original jurisdiction over all offenses against the laws of the United States not punishable by death or imprisonment at hard labor. By the same act, the Chickasaw Nation and a greater portion of the Choctaw Nation as far north as the Canadian River was annexed to the Eastern Judicial District of Texas, at Paris, and this court was given jurisdiction over all federal law violations in this part of the territory not given to the new court at Muskogee.

Finally, in 1895, Congress divided Indian Territory into three judicial districts—Northern, Central, and Southern. The Northern District included the Quapaw Agency and the area of the Creek and Cherokee nations, with headquarters at Muskogee and court towns at Vinita, Miami, and Tahlequah; the Central District embraced the Choctaw Nation, with headquarters at McAlester and courts at Atoka, Antlers, and Cameron; and the Southern District comprised the Seminole and Chickasaw nations, with headquarters at Ardmore and courts at Purcell, Pauls Valley, Chickasha, and Ryan. Through a special provision the three district judges acted as a court of appeals, presided over by the senior judge acting as chief justice, to which decisions of any of the trial courts could be appealed, and McAlester was designated as the seat of the appellate court. In the next few years, Congress provided for holding terms of court in other towns, including Durant and Tishomingo.

Meanwhile, additional railroads were being built that linked the Indian nations more closely; settlers and speculators poured in from every direction, and towns sprang up faster than the townsite commissions could survey and appraise them. The Atoka Agreement for the Chickasaws and Choctaws and the Curtis Act for the Five Civilized Tribes had become effective in 1897. The Dawes Commission proceeded with tribal rolls and allotments in severalty, the tribal courts were abolished, and the laws of Arkansas extended over the territory as far as practicable. The Atoka Agreement provided that certain lands could be reserved for townsite and cemetery purposes and not allotted to Chickasaw and Choctaw citizens, and that townsite commissions under supervision of the Dawes Commission should perform the duty of setting aside and officially laying off into streets, alleys, blocks, and lots towns of more than two hundred population.

The triangle formed by Durant, Madill, and Tishomingo on the Washita River was dotted with settlements of considerable size and antiquity. Ten miles east of Tishomingo, on the Choctaw, Oklahoma and Gulf Railway, Milburn had been born in 1901. South and east were Emet, Bee, and

63

Nida, and across the Washita was Linn, on the road to Madill. It was forty-five miles west to Ardmore, the largest town in the Chickasaw Nation in 1906.

So Indian Territory was in ferment, with the old order slowly passing and the new order not yet established.

There were drawbacks to life in this land of promise. Fugitives and undesirables, many of them from Texas, had found anonymity and a haven from the law. Although they were a minority, they gave the country a bad name. Bootleggers were thick, and not all the vast quantities of Peruna and the extracts sold by stores went for medicinal and cooking purposes.

The only law enforcement outside the towns was still provided by the United States marshals, their deputies, and the Indian Police. Less than a dozen of these officers served the region between Durant and Ardmore. One was Ben Collins.

Collins lived on a little farm at Emet, five miles south of Milburn. He was a young man of fine build, and was known as a daring officer. He had served as a United States Indian policeman and deputy marshal since 1898. In this capacity, he had made many sensational arrests and also acquired a number of enemies. One was Port Pruitt, a prominent citizen of Orr.

While attempting to arrest Pruitt at a Fourth of July celebration in 1903, Collins had shot him, and as a result, Pruitt remained partially paralyzed. Pruitt charged Collins with assault to kill, but the case was dismissed in the United States Commissioner's Court at Ardmore. Port's brother, Clint, a well-to-do citizen of Cornish, joined the fight. The Pruitts swore they would "get Ben Collins."

Months passed. The affair seemed to have been forgotten until the summer of 1905. A notorious gunman, who happened to be a friend of Collins, came to Ben and told him: "I've been offered $500 to kill you." He showed Collins a check for $200 drawn on a bank at Madill and said, "The other $300 is to be paid when the job is done."

"What are you going to do about it?" Collins asked.

The gunman laughed. "Hell, Ben, I wouldn't shoot you for that and you know it! I'm going to cash this check and leave the country." And he did.

Then about noon, July 17, 1906, a man named Ahmed Washmood appeared at the Collins place in a buggy. Of "heavy physique, florid complexion, strong features, keen blue eyes and dark brown hair without a vestige of gray," he "presented a natty appearance" and represented himself as an insurance agent from Texas. He wanted to see Ben. When told that Ben wasn't home, he asked for dinner and feed for his horses. Mrs. Collins gave him dinner, and her hired boy fed the team. Washmood stated that his headquarters were in Durant, but that he was thinking about going "further west" and had a proposition he thought might interest Collins. Most of his conversation was with the hired boy.

Mrs. Collins next saw him that evening about dark at the pasture gate, talking to her husband. He asked Collins to travel with him west of Ardmore where Ben knew the country, offering him five dollars a day and expenses. Collins sensed a trap and declined.

Two weeks later, Washmood came to the house again. He said he was leaving for the west and wanted to know if Collins had changed his mind. The hired boy told him that Ben was on official business in the Washita bottoms and was not expected to return until late Wednesday night.

On Wednesday morning, August 1, Washmood stopped at Doc Thomas' hotel in Emet and asked to use the tele-

65

phone. Thomas remembered his conversation as follows: " 'I want Mr. Alford at the Rock Hotel in Madill.' In a few minutes the bell rang again and he said: 'Is that you?' and then 'Yes,' and he said, 'The party has been located and everything is ready. Meet me this evening between sundown and dark at Linn.' "

Washmood was next seen at dusk on the road west of Emet by Dr. Earl Peachland of Tishomingo. "He was in a yellow-wheeled buggy and driving a brown team," Dr. Peachland recalled. "He stopped me and asked the way to Bee and across the Washita to Linn. Later he stated that he believed he would stay at Emet that night and go to Bee the next morning."

Collins spent the day placing an allottee in possession of his land on the Washita. Mrs. Collins and the hired boy had finished supper and retired to the front porch to wait for her husband. At nine o'clock, they heard a horse coming up the rocky trail by the pasture, and the boy said, "That's Ben now."

In a moment the sounds died, and Mrs. Collins remarked: "That isn't Ben. That horse turned off at the gate." The road forked at the gate, and the main trail went on to Emet.

In a few minutes, they heard a second horse on the trail. "That's Ben," Mrs. Collins said. She recognized his horse by its peculiar gait. She stood on the porch, waiting for him to appear from the darkness.

Suddenly the heavy blast of a shotgun shattered the evening quiet. Immediately afterward, four lighter shots were fired almost simultaneously. The shotgun roared again, then hoofbeats drummed away in the night.

Mrs. Collins rushed into the house and grabbed her pistol. She heard Ben scream as she ran down the road. The hired boy ran ahead of her, telling her to go back, but she ran on.

Ben lay on the ground beside the gate. She lifted his head and "tried to get him to speak," but Ben Collins was dead. A load of No. 8 buckshot had caught him in the abdomen, knocking him from the saddle. The other shot had struck him in the face, tearing his left cheek from his nose. His revolver was in his right hand. Four empty shells in its cylinder showed he had tried valiantly to defend himself.

News of the killing reached United States Marshal Jones at Tishomingo by telephone. The whole community was aroused. Jones cautioned the people not to go tramping around the scene. Dr. J. H. Bridges drove to Emet to conduct the official examination and care for the remains.

At daybreak, Bridges and George Turnbull, an Indian deputy, picked up some horse tracks about fifty yards north of the pasture gate and followed them half a mile. The horse was shod, and they noted that one shoe was longer than the rest. In a clump of brush just off the trail, they found the freshly cut wheel marks of a buggy. Ground signs showed that the horse had been hitched to the back of the buggy. A second horse hitched to the buggy was not shod, and Turnbull noted that its right hind hoof left a peculiar gap in the track. There were footprints of two men in the brush. The buggy had gone west.

Two miles west of Emet, Will Stevens had heard shooting in the direction of the Collins place. He was standing in his front yard and saw the rig pass hurriedly at 9:35 P.M. "There were two men in the buggy. Looked to be a brown team," he said. Turnbull and Bridges tracked the vehicle to Tishomingo.

P. W. Martin, who operated a livery stable at Tishomingo, told Bridges and Turnbull: "I hired a yellow-wheeled rig to Washmood about 3 o'clock yesterday. It was a brown team. One on the right a horse and shod and the one on the left a mare, unshod. He said he would bring the team back that evening, but didn't bring them back till this morning." They had been driven hard. Washmood was alone.

Bridges examined the team. He found a piece broken from the right hind hoof of the mare, accounting for the "peculiar gap" in her track. The left hind hoof of the horse wore an extra-long shoe. Bridges had the shoe removed from the horse. He then returned to the Collins place and "fitted it to the tracks exactly."

Mrs. Armstrong, at the Tishomingo Hotel, supplied the additional information that put the marshals on Washmood's trail:

He came here late Tuesday and wanted a room. He retired and I saw him the next morning. He asked if he could get rooms for a couple of friends that night. About 4 o'clock he came to the hotel and said he was going to the country and would be back that evening. No friends came to rent any rooms, his room had not been occupied, and I didn't see him again until 9 o'clock this morning. He came after his grip and asked about the train to Ardmore.

Washmood reached Ardmore that afternoon. Friday morning, August 3, Ardmore officers found his name on the register at the Gilmer Hotel. When they went to his room, however, he was gone. Upon inquiry, they were told he had left for Durant that morning on the six o'clock Frisco.

Friday evening, Deputy A. N. Wilcox arrested Washmood as he stepped off the train at Durant.

At first he stated that he knew who had murdered Ben Collins. Then he denied everything. He had started to Linn to sell some insurance but had met his party on the road. He knew the man only as "Mr. Alford." He was accompanied by an Indian whom Washmood had never seen before. They had asked to borrow his rig for the evening. The Indian had returned it to him at Emet.

"I didn't learn of the killing till I got to Tishomingo," Washmood said.

But, Doc Thomas told officers:

Washmood knew about the killing before that. He came to my place about 10:30 or 11 o'clock, after the shooting. I had gone to bed but got up to smoke. As I was filling my pipe, I heard the clock strike distinctly ten times. I then smoked a while and went back to bed. He came after I had gone to sleep. He stated it was early yet, only 9 o'clock. I informed him it was well after ten and nearly eleven. He wanted to spend the night. He had stayed with me a couple of times before.

He retired, and I noticed that he was very restless. I arose about 5 A.M., and Washmood was already up. Ed Collins came and started talking about Ben's death. Washmood got very nervous—most nervous man I ever saw. He turned as pale as death, and left soon afterwards.

The government charged Washmood with murder. United States Commissioner Etling, of Durant, held the examining trial at 2:30 P.M., August 11.

Details of the hearing appear in the Durant *Daily News* of August 12, 1906:

Long before the trial began the courtroom was packed. Dressed in deep black . . . Mrs. Collins came slowly into the room shortly after 1 o'clock and many words of sympathy were heard on every hand. Washmood came in with Deputy Wilcox at 1:30. An audible sob and a craning of necks as his name passed the lips of the audience was the only visible demonstration. In shirt sleeves, without tie or collar, and his hair damp with perspiration, he no longer presented a trim and natty appearance. He took a seat between his lawyers Kyle and Crook, of this city, and immediately entered into deep conversation with them.

When court opened, his lawyers waived arraignment and entered a plea of not guilty. . . .

After Commissioner Etling had instructed the witnesses, the prosecuting attorney Z. E. Utterback called Mrs. Collins to the stand to relate the death of her husband. Though her great black eyes showed the pain which the recital gave her, she did not falter, nor did she cry in the telling. . . .

The other witnesses followed to the chair and told their stories. This closed the testimony for the prosecution. The defense offered none.

Attorney Crook arose and made an eloquent, dramatic plea for the liberty of his client. He reviewed the testimony and challenged the court to bring forth one iota of evidence therein which would tend to show the defendant as the slayer of Ben Collins.

Commissioner Etling ruled that the prisoner should be held without bail until the next term of the United States court. Washmood was transferred to the federal jail at Ardmore.

Immediately his attorneys began a series of maneuvers to obtain his release. They applied to Judge Hosea Townsend of the Southern District for a writ of habeas corpus. But Judge Townsend happened to be out of his district, and the petition was brought to Chickasha in the court of Judge J. T. Dickerson, who had coextensive jurisdiction when Townsend was absent. Judge Dickerson refused to hear the petition, stating that the matter would have to wait until Townsend returned.

The attorneys then filed a damage suit of five hundred dollars against Dickerson and asked for a trial before Judge W. H. H. Clayton of the Central District at McAlester. The suit was finally dismissed. Judge Townsend returned to his district, held a hearing on the habeas corpus writ, and ordered Washmood released because, although some interesting evidence had been developed at the preliminary hearing, "nothing was learned which had a direct bearing on the charge of murder."

The Chickasaw National Council appropriated one thousand dollars for the arrest and conviction of Ben Collins' killer. The family employed private detectives to work with the federal officers. Within a few weeks, they had identified "Mr. Alford" of Madill as Jim Miller, arrested Dan Sie as the Indian who had accompanied Miller the night of the killing and returned the buggy to Washmood at Emet, and determined that Washmood had "set up the plot" and delivered to Miller, at Ardmore, "$1,800 furnished by Clint Pruitt."

In October, 1906, a federal grand jury returned murder indictments against Miller, Dan Sie, Pruitt, and Washmood. Dan Sie was in jail, Pruitt was arrested by deputy marshals at his home near Cornish, and Washmood was returned from Texas on a fugitive warrant from the Southern District of Indian Territory.

The trial was called at Tishomingo. Each defendant got a change of venue to Ardmore. Ardmore authorities sent the case back to Tishomingo as the district where the crime had been committed. The Tishomingo district judge transferred the case to Ardmore again on the ground that a change of venue had been granted and therefore his court had no jurisdiction. Eventually, all three defendants were out on bail.

It was the greatest piece of legal hocus-pocus in the history of the territory. Time and the grim reaper were to play the final role in the Collins case.

Dan Sie died from natural causes. Clint Pruitt was slain

in a gun fight with Officer Tom Gilstrap on the streets of Cornish. Three years later, after many of the key witnesses had died or could not be located, Washmood stood trial at Ardmore.

He "plead an alibi and proved that he had not participated in the actual killing." Despite this evidence, the jury found him "guilty as charged" in the original indictment. His lawyer immediately filed a motion for a new trial. The motion was heard by the court the same afternoon Washmood was convicted, and the case was set aside because "the testimony was not sufficient to support such a verdict."

Miller was the foxy one. Before Washmood was released on the writ of habeas corpus, Deacon Jim began covering his back trail. Despite his precautions, detectives traced him from Ardmore to Fort Worth, northwest to his old stamping grounds in Hall County, east across old Greer County, and into the Kiowa-Comanche country of southwestern Oklahoma Territory which had been opened to settlement in 1901.

On the morning of December 4, 1906, United States Marshal John Abernathy of Guthrie, Deputy Marshal Frank Canton, and Kiowa County Deputy Sheriffs John Harris and Jesse Morris surrounded the residence of Miller's sister in Hobart. Deacon Jim was hiding there. They sent a friend to the door to tell him to surrender. Deacon Jim appeared in the doorway with a revolver in his hand. His friend told him the officers were armed with Winchesters and were determined to take him, dead or alive. Quietly, Miller handed over his weapon.

"I've got out of other scrapes," he remarked, "and I reckon I will this one."

Abernathy and Canton arrived in Guthrie with their prisoner on December 6. The next day, the *Oklahoma State*

72

Capital described Miller as "a gentleman tough" and a "Texas outlaw who has escaped several courts," and added, "He is a peculiar character and boasts that he never gives up to an officer unless he first gets the consent of his own mind. He is also peculiar in his habits. He neither chews, smokes or drinks whiskey."

Miller was transferred to Tishomingo for his preliminary hearing in January, ordered held without bond, and lodged in jail at Ardmore. Late in 1907, with one of his conspirators already dead, some of the witnesses disappeared, and no prospect for an early trial, he was admitted to bail by Judge Townsend.

Deacon Jim went back to Fort Worth. He arrived in time to answer a summons from his old friend and brother-in-law, Mannie Clements, now a constable at El Paso. Carl Adamson, their New Mexico relative, had sent word for Jim to come to Las Cruces.

Another man had been marked for death—the famed former sheriff, Patrick Floyd Garrett. The price was fifteen hundred dollars.

9. Goats and Cattle

ALTHOUGH it had been more than twenty-five years since Pat Garrett had killed Billy the Kid in Lucien B. Maxwell's house at Fort Sumner, he was still the most widely known man in New Mexico and the subject of much controversy.

He had been severely criticized for shooting the Kid in the darkness without warning, and the deed was considered all the uglier because the two had once been friends. Most of the criticism came from the Kid's sympathizers, but they exerted enough influence in Lincoln County to prevent Garrett's renomination for sheriff.

Pat bought a ranch on Eagle Creek in the Sierra Blanca Mountains and did well for a couple of years. In 1884, he was commissioned by Governor John Ireland of Texas as captain of a Ranger company to combat cattle thieves along the Texas–New Mexico border. He sold his ranch to an Englishman, Brandon Kirby. When his tour of duty with the Rangers ended, he became manager of the enlarged Kirby holdings. In June, 1887, he moved to Roswell and acquired some land on the Hondo River, organizing a corporation known as the Pecos Valley Ditch Company of Lincoln County. Its purpose was to irrigate the valley with water from artesian wells and the Hondo.

Garrett promoted his company and dabbled in real estate until the new county of Chaves was created, then ran for sheriff. He was sorely defeated. Disgruntled and bitter from this obvious lack of appreciation for his past efforts, he disposed of his holdings in New Mexico and went to Uvalde, Texas.

At Uvalde, he bred and raised Quarter Horses and Thoroughbreds, racing them at tracks in Texas and Louisiana. It would have been a successful business venture, and Pat might have lived out his days and slept under the live oaks along the Leon River, except for his weakness for gambling. He soon lost the small fortune he had acquired.

His need for money caused him to return to New Mexico in the spring of 1896. On February 1, Colonel Albert J. Fountain, chief investigator and prosecutor for the Southeastern New Mexico Stock Growers' Association, and his eight-year-old son disappeared and were undoubtedly murdered at Chalk Hill, near White Sands, on the Tularosa–Las Cruces road. News of their disappearance appeared in newspapers throughout the Southwest, and public indignation spread until the aggregate bounty for the arrest and conviction of the killers and recovery of the bodies totaled twenty thousand dollars. It was the richest reward ever offered in the annals of crime in the West, and Pat accepted Governor William T. Thornton's invitation to try to solve the mystery. He put on the sheriff's star in Doña Ana County on March 22, to finish an unexpired term, then was elected to a full term in 1898.

Pat plunged immediately into his primary task. His investigations led to warrants being issued for the arrest of Oliver Lee, a prominent rancher, William McNew, and James Gilliland. Pat arrested McNew. Capturing Lee and Gilliland was another matter. They killed one of Pat's deputies in a gun battle with his posse at Wildy Well Ranch, then hid out in the vast Tularosa Basin country until they were ready to surrender. Lee and Gilliland stood trial at Hillsboro for eighteen days during May and June of 1899. They were defended by Albert Bacon Fall, later to be involved in the Teapot Dome scandal, and prosecuted by Thomas Benton Catron, of the "Santa Fe Ring," a bitter political enemy of Oliver Lee. In this test of strength between the territory's two most powerful politicians, Fall and Catron, Pat came out on the losing side. Lee and Gilliland were acquitted.

Garrett remained at Las Cruces until his term as sheriff expired. On December 20, 1901, President Theodore Roosevelt appointed him collector of customs at El Paso. In 1905, Pat was the special guest of the President at the Rough Riders Reunion in San Antonio, where he misrepresented his pal, Tom Powers, an El Paso saloonkeeper, to Roosevelt as one of the biggest cattlemen in West Texas. This breach of etiquette, together with numerous complaints from El Paso's reform element about Pat's playing poker and following the races, discredited him with the President. When his term ended on January 1, 1906, Roosevelt appointed another candidate.

Pat returned to Doña Ana County. He had acquired a little ranch on the eastern slopes of the Organ Mountains, about twenty miles from Las Cruces. It was a pleasant place set between two hills at the very base of the range and five miles north of the road through San Augustine Pass which led into the Tularosa Basin, considered by Oliver Lee and his friends as their private domain. It was good range land, and there was an excellent spring above Pat's house which the Basin ranchers coveted. Pat invested what money he had in some brood mares and stallions, hoping to get back into the business of breeding racing stock. But it was no secret that he was interested in completing the job he had begun in 1896. The Fountain case reward money was still available, and he was determined to vindicate himself of the shame he had suffered from his failure to bring in the Fountain killers. The Basin spread before him thirty miles to the Jarillas and Sacramentos, and the San Augustine ranch of W. W. Cox, Lee's brother-in-law, was up in the Organs within spyglass distance of Garrett's Bear Canyon pasture. All this irritated the Lee gang, and one complication followed another.

Pat's horse-breeding operation did not turn out well, and he became hard pressed financially. He had not been able to pay his taxes, and he owed a Las Cruces merchant three thousand dollars. The merchant agreed to take two thousand for the debt, and Cox offered to lend Garrett this amount. Pat took it as a neighborly act and gave Cox a mortgage on his ranch and stock. Negligently or not, Cox allowed the mortgage to lapse, and the sheriff, holding a fistful of tax warrants, seized and sold Pat's stock under attachment.

The sheriff did not find all the stock; Garrett had put some of his cattle and best brood mares on Cox's range and branded them in the San Augustine brand to keep them out of the way. When Cox failed to get his money, he refused to give up Pat's horses and cattle. He offered to buy the ranch, but Pat refused to sell, so Cox went to Oliver Lee for advice. Lee suggested, "We'll goat him off."

A few weeks later, Wayne Brazil, who had worked for Cox at one time, came to Garrett and offered to lease his

Bear Canyon pasture for grazing purposes. Brazil was thirty years old and a typical cowboy. He was of strong build and had sandy hair, rough features, and a ruddy complexion. He wore a black broad-brimmed hat, the crown pushed up high, pulled well over his ears. A scar ran from the right corner of his mouth to the base of his chin—a souvenir of an old knife fight. But he had no gun record. In fact, he was "never in the habit of going armed." Pat considered him a good-natured, slow-moving fellow. He had known Brazil as a boy when he lived at Lincoln; Wayne's father, W. W. Brazil, had helped Garrett capture Billy the Kid. Pat suspected nothing. As he did not have enough stock for his Bear Canyon pasture, he accepted Brazil's proposition.

Shortly after the lease agreement was signed, Brazil stocked the range with goats. Garrett was surprised and indignant. He knew that goats and sheep would ruin his range for horses and cattle, and he accused Brazil of acting in bad faith. Brazil had told him he was bringing in three hundred to four hundred cattle, but the contract failed to specify what kind of stock he was to run on the Bear Canyon property. Sheep would not have been unusual, but goats were. Where had Brazil acquired them, when goat raisers in that part of the country were practically nonexistent? He gave Pat no satisfactory answer.

Garrett thought about suing Brazil for breach of contract. His lawyers told him that his only course was to buy Brazil out or get him to transfer the lease. In January, 1908, Pat had Brazil arrested under an old statute that forbade keeping livestock within one and one-half miles of a ranch house or settlement. This action didn't work either. The justice of the peace dismissed his complaint for lack of evidence. Pat grew desperate. He had to get Brazil off his range, or it would be worthless for any future transactions.

His first ray of hope came in mid-February, 1908. Jim Miller and Carl Adamson appeared in Las Cruces posing as cattlemen. Both were strangers in the area.

Adamson did the talking around town. He passed word that Miller was seeking grazing land for a thousand head of cattle he was bringing from Mexico. He contrived to meet Garrett and immediately offered to lease his entire ranch, including the goat-ridden Bear Canyon. The Mexican cattle were to be delivered in El Paso on March 15. Garrett would be paid so much a head until fall, at which time the cattle would be transferred to Miller's ranch in Oklahoma. Garrett considered the offer attractive. The deal could not be consummated, however, unless they could come to terms with Brazil for the removal of his goats.

Adamson talked as if his partner had a buyer for the goats, and Garrett arranged a meeting with Brazil. Brazil agreed to sell twelve hundred goats at $3.50 each and surrender the lease. A few days later, Brazil announced that he had eighteen hundred goats instead of twelve hundred. Garrett explained the situation to Adamson—his tenant had miscalculated the size of his herd by one-third. Adamson supposedly consulted with Miller and reported back to Garrett. The buyer would take twelve hundred goats, but was unable to handle the others. Brazil then told Garrett that he would not get off the ranch until he had sold the entire herd.

Garrett allegedly became hostile, abused Brazil verbally, and finally slapped his face, thus providing a motive for what happened afterward.

Garrett, Adamson, and Brazil met at Garrett's ranch the evening of February 28 and discussed the entire matter. After hours of futile wrangling, they agreed on only one point—the thing had to be settled the next day or not at all.

79

Adamson suggested that all three of them go to Las Cruces and talk to Miller.

Adamson remained at the ranch that night. Mrs. Garrett was apprehensive and expressed her suspicions to her husband; Pat shrugged them off. Adamson was a little too persuasive perhaps, but everything seemed on the square. Pat had no reason to believe that his life was in danger.

Early the next morning, he and Adamson started for Las Cruces in a buggy. Garrett held the reins in his gloved hands. Adamson rode in the seat beside him. On the floor between them rested Pat's ten-gauge "folding" shotgun, loaded with bird shot. The barrels were detached and slid, together with the stock, into a leather case. The gun could be easily assembled for use. In placing it in the buggy, Pat had remarked, "I might shoot something for the family pot before I get back." Otherwise, he was unarmed.

Pat was dressed in his best black broadcloth suit and string tie. "This Miller sounds like somebody important," he had told his wife, "and I don't want him to think I'm plumb down on my luck."

Garrett had never seen Miller. Some authorities claim the two men were acquainted—that they had met when Miller was a deputy sheriff in West Texas. During these years, Pat was living at Uvalde and racing horses in Louisiana, hundreds of miles away. It is likely he had heard or read of Miller's exploits, but he probably failed to associate "Killer" Miller with Miller the cattleman whom he was going to see. Perhaps his anxiety to rid himself of Brazil's goat herd clouded his memory. Otherwise, it is hard to believe that an old gunfighter like Garrett, even with age upon him, his eyes growing dim, and his trigger finger losing its quickness, would have allowed himself to be cold-bloodedly maneuvered into a position from which there was but one exit.

80

It was a four-hour drive to Las Cruces. The buggy crawled up the long slope to the top of San Augustine Pass. As the road dipped downward, Wayne Brazil joined them on horseback. He carried a .45 Colt on his right hip and a Winchester rifle strapped to his saddle. Brazil's sudden display of weapons, even if Garrett took note of them, was no cause for alarm. Men who ordinarily never packed firearms often armed themselves for long trips across country.

Around midmorning, the three-man party passed through the little mining camp of Organ. Some loungers in front of L. B. Bentley's store and post office heard them "jawing at each other" over Brazil's goats.

After leaving Organ, the country was wide open. The road traversed a sloping mesa for about ten miles, then dropped sharply through a series of foothills which ended a few miles from Las Cruces in the Mesilla Valley. In these foothills, at a point sheltered from view on all sides, the goat argument, according to Adamson and Brazil, reached its climax. Sheriff Felipe Lucero, in an article written by Margaret Page Hood for the *New Mexico Sentinel* of April 23, 1939, explained what happened:

I was getting ready to go to lunch when the door at the sheriff's office opened and in walked Wayne Brazil, looking harried and upset. He had his gun in his hand, and as he came up to my desk he laid it down in front of me. "Lock me up," he said, "I've just killed Pat Garrett!" I laughed and asked him, "What are you trying to do, Wayne, josh me?" But he insisted he'd just killed Garrett with his .45 out on the Organ road. I gave him a second look and saw he wasn't joking. I put his gun in the safe and locked him up in a cell.

I put his horse in the stable where we kept our mounts, and untied my own. Already Wayne had told me where I'd find Garrett, lying dead in a sandy arroyo about four miles east of town.

"The man who was with Pat when I killed him," Wayne told me, "is outside the jail sitting in Pat's buggy. He's a man named Adamson, and he saw the whole thing and knows I shot in self-defense."

Sure enough, I found this Adamson waiting for me. He followed me while I summoned a coroner's jury, then trailed when I led the way to the scene of the shooting.

Adamson related his version of the killing en route. He told how they had overtaken Brazil on the other side of Organ. Brazil "rode along by the buggy on the right side," sometimes to the rear, sometimes to the front. Brazil's goats and the terms of the lease were discussed, and as the argument grew warm, "we stopped to fix the harness."

Adamson did not say whether the harness was merely disarranged or broken:

I got out of the buggy to fix it, and while I was standing there, I heard Garrett say to Brazil, "I don't give a damn whether you sell all your goats or not. I can get you off anyway; I'll put you off right now." He then leaped from the buggy. I don't know whether he grabbed his gun as he did so, or got his gun after Brazil shot him and before he fell. I did not see as I was on the other side of the horses. I know that when Garrett fell he dropped his gun, and it had not been fired. I am sure he thought he could cover Brazil with his shotgun before Brazil could draw the Winchester, and so did not count on Brazil's revolver—as Brazil rode on the right side of the buggy, I am sure that Garrett did not know that he had a revolver. . . . As Garrett fell on the ground, he was dead. There were two bullet holes in his body; I am not positive whether the first shot hit him in the back of the head or the breast. I stepped from behind the rig just as he fell, and Brazil got off his horse and said: "This is hell!" He handed me his revolver, and got into the buggy. I put a lap robe over the corpse, hitched Brazil's horse behind, and we drove to Las Cruces.

Sheriff Lucero and the jury reached the spot where the buggy had halted in a six-inch drift of sand at the roadside. Garrett's long, rangy figure lay flat on its back, one leg drawn up, his shotgun nearby.

We could plainly see the wheel tracks and the impression of the horses' hoofs in the sand, the depressions they'd made when they'd plunged at the sound of the shots. I trailed the tracks back two miles. It was plain to see the team and [Brazil's] horse had been walked side by side, the men apparently talking together as they rode.

Dr. W. C. Field, according to the *Sentinel* interview, reached the scene only minutes behind Sheriff Lucero:

I made a careful examination of the body. . . . Pat's clothes were open and disarranged [the fly on his trousers was unbuttoned], showing that he had gotten from the buggy to relieve himself at the time he was killed. He'd taken the glove from his left hand, but a heavy driving glove was still on his right hand. I couldn't help but ponder that point.

A man as wise in such matters as Pat . . . who took infinite precautions in his shooting of Billy the Kid . . . wouldn't have been in the position he had probably been in, wouldn't have turned his back, if he'd thought he was in danger. . . .

His shotgun lay parallel to his body about three feet from him, in its scabbard. It lay without any sand kicked up around it. That was another point I noticed. When a man's shot in the back of the head, the way Pat was, he does one of two things with whatever he has in his hand. Either he clutches it convulsively tight or he throws it wide. There were no signs in the sand that the gun had been violently thrown. It was placed near the body after he was killed. . . .

Later, at the undertaking parlor, I made an autopsy on Pat. He'd been shot twice by soft-nosed bullets, one shot hitting him in the back of the head and emerging just over the right eye. I was sure he'd been shot in the back of the head because when I examined the hole I noticed his long hair was driven into the wound. The second shot was fired when Pat was on the ground, the bullet striking in the region of the stomach and ranging upward. I cut this bullet out behind the shoulder. It was a .45.

The jury issued a formal verdict stating merely that the deceased had come to his death at the hands of Wayne Brazil. The following Monday, March 2, Dudley Poe Garrett, Pat's son, officially charged Brazil with murder.

The preliminary hearing was held on Wednesday afternoon before Justice of the Peace Manuel López. The Doña Ana County courtroom was crowded with Garrett's many friends, including Governor George Curry, Attorney General James M. Hervey, and Fred Fornoff, captain of the Territorial Mounted Police, who had rushed to Las Cruces from Santa Fe upon receiving word of Garrett's death. Brazil occupied the prisoner's chair, facing the justice. He was accompanied in court by W. W. Cox, who became his close companion in the days that followed, and the attorney for the defense, Albert Bacon Fall. District Attorney Mark B. Thompson appeared for the territory. The bereaved widow was not present, but a few feet away sat Dudley Garrett and his sisters, Anne and Elizabeth.

Brazil's version of the shooting was brief and simple: "Garrett kept telling me he'd put me off his land. He leaned over the buggy; I saw him reach for his shotgun, so I shot him twice."

Adamson, the only witness to the tragedy, testified that he was a comparative stranger to both defendant and deceased, that he had accompanied them to Las Cruces to arrange for the purchase of Brazil's goats. He did not mention Miller's name. Under oath, he changed his story somewhat in repeating the conversation between Brazil and Garrett:

They kept arguing. . . . Garrett was angry, and said to Brazil, "I don't care whether you give up the ranch or not; I'll get you off anyway!" About that time he stopped the buggy for a certain purpose, and I took the lines. He was standing beside the buggy and I heard him say, "Damn you, I'll get you off now," or something like that. Brazil was on his horse at my back. I did not hear what else was said, but when I heard the shots I turned and saw Garrett on the ground. . . . Brazil had his six-shooter in his hand. Garrett was dead when I got to him; his shotgun was by his side. He never spoke, but groaned a little.

Asked if at any time he had seen the shotgun in Garrett's hand, Adamson said: "I don't know anything about it. I wasn't looking that way."

A Doña Ana County grand jury indicted Wayne Brazil on April 13, 1908. He was released on ten thousand dollars' bail furnished by Cox and friends of Oliver Lee. A few weeks later, Mrs. Garrett, in order to maintain her family, sold the Organ Mountain ranch for what equity Pat had in it. The buyer, of course, was W. W. Cox.

Meanwhile, Governor Curry, a long-time friend of Garrett and thoroughly familiar with the unfriendly feelings of Cox, Lee, and their mountain-ranching friends toward the former sheriff, made numerous inquiries privately and publicly to discover a deeper motive for his death. Attorney General Hervey probed the findings of Sheriff Lucero and Dr. Fields and "directed searching questions" to Adamson and Brazil at the preliminary hearing and inquest.

If Garrett had been taking his gun from the buggy, why

was his back turned to Brazil when the first shot was fired? Stranger still, why would a man of Pat's experience and skill with firearms, in a quarrel, permit his antagonist to get the drop on him? Did not the unbuttoned fly on his trousers and his ungloved left hand show that he had gotten out of the buggy for another purpose, that he was not expecting trouble at the time and had made no preparations for defense? Even if Brazil's story was true, why had the second shot been necessary?

These questions broadened into what Garrett's friends deemed a well-formulated plot when Captain Fornoff made an investigation of the scene. A short distance from the road, in the hills, he found a spot trampled by the hoofs of a horse, presumably with a rider. Horse droppings scattered about showed that the rider had waited there for some time. Under a bush nearby he found two .44 Winchester shells. In his opinion, the real assassin had stood behind the bush and shot at least one bullet into the back of Garrett's head as he stood beside the buggy; as Pat lay on the ground, dead or dying, Brazil had fired a .45 slug into his stomach.

Fornoff never believed the murder happened just as Adamson stated—especially after he learned that, for two weeks prior to the slaying, Miller, in his preacherlike garb, had been seen on mysterious business in White Oaks, Tularosa, and San Augustine Pass and that on the morning of the killing he had been seen in a Las Cruces bank and at the Park Hotel. Fornoff knew Adamson and knew of his criminal record. He also knew the record of Jim Miller and that he and Adamson were related.

All these findings prompted Governor Curry to write: "If Captain Fornoff had been able to employ competent secret service men, I am confident he would have been able to

John Wesley Hardin studied law in prison and was admitted to the bar upon his return to Gonzales County. He went to El Paso as a special attorney for Jim Miller to aid in the prosecution of Frazer.

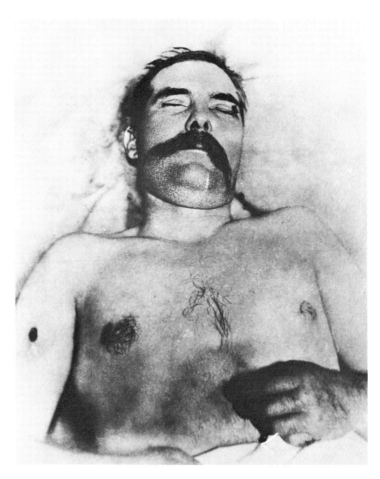

Hardin was unable to help his relative Jim Miller at Frazer's trial in Mitchell County. He was shot and killed by Constable John Selman in the Acme Saloon at El Paso on August 19, 1895.

Ben Collins with relatives and friends. Seated, l. to r.: Ben Collins; Dan Collins, father of Ben and Dan, Jr.; Corn Colbert. Standing, l. to r.: ———, Dan Collins, Jr., ———.

Courtesy Dan H. Collins, Austin, Texas

Patrick Floyd Garrett,
the tall slayer of Billy the Kid,
was shot and killed near
Las Cruces, New Mexico,
on February 29, 1908.

From author's collection

Fred Fornoff, captain of the New Mexico Mounted Police, investigated the slaying of Patrick Floyd Garrett. He always believed the real killer was Jim Miller.

Courtesy Division of Manuscripts,
University of Oklahoma Libraries

Moman Pruiett, noted criminal lawyer, whose name was sacred to the criminal element of Ada, Oklahoma. When Miller announced that he had hired Pruiett to defend him and his partners, Ada citizens took matters into their own hands.

Courtesy Division of Manuscripts,
University of Oklahoma Libraries

At rope's end in Ada, Oklahoma, on April 19, 1909. Hanging,
l. to r.: Jim Miller, Joe Allen, B. B. Burrell, Jesse West.

From author's collection

A report of the lynching in an Ada newspaper. Note the improper spelling of Burrell's name in the headlines.

From author's collection

develop the facts in this case. The Territory did not have funds available for such an investigation."

None of this evidence was presented at Brazil's trial on April 19, 1909. District Attorney Thompson made "only a perfunctory effort" at prosecution. Afterward and for several years, he was Albert Fall's personal attorney. The case was tried before Judge Frank W. Parker, who, ten years before, had presided at the trial of Oliver Lee in Hillsboro. Carl Adamson, who was available, was not called to testify by either the prosecution or the defense. Nor did anyone appear to be interested in the possible testimony of Jim Miller. Sheriff Lucero, Dr. Field, and four members of the coroner's jury were put on the stand just long enough to establish that Garrett had been slain.

According to Dr. Field, in the *New Mexico Sentinel*, "I made a careful record of everything I'd found and told the district attorney so. He said, 'I'll ask for what I want on the witness stand.' Well, I never gave that testimony in detail, because I wasn't questioned! Maybe he didn't think a country doctor's testimony was important."

Brazil, the only other witness, stuck to his story of self-defense. Asked, on cross-examination, why he had fired the second shot, he remembered: "Adamson shouted to me, 'Don't shoot him again,' but I was so keyed up I couldn't stop myself."

Attorney Fall thought Brazil's explanation was sufficient to convince the jury. He was right. With no evidence to substantiate a charge of murder, the jury returned a verdict of acquittal in fifteen minutes.

Carl Adamson wasn't so lucky. In June, 1908, he was caught smuggling a wagonload of Chinese into the United States from the Republic of Mexico. He was indicted in the

Sixth Judicial District of the territory, and tried at Alamo-gordo. The jury found him guilty, and on December 14 he was sentenced to serve one and one-half years in prison.

Smuggling Chinese was considered one of the lowest of criminal endeavors. As an old cowpuncher in White Oaks put it, "Hell, I'd rather be caught trying to steal a wagonload of calves; it would be a damn sight more respectable."

Nine of every ten old-timers in New Mexico believed that Adamson had deliberately arranged the trip to Las Cruces. It developed that Miller had no herd of cattle that would require pasturage on March 15. He had no ranch in Okla-homa and no buyer for Brazil's goats. Many whispered that the entire plot was hatched in a lawyer's office at El Paso, with the cattlemen who wanted Garrett out of the way agree-ing to supply someone to take the blame for the murder. They said Brazil was paid five hundred dollars for the role, and they pointed to the big barbecue that was held at W. W. Cox's San Augustine ranch to celebrate Brazil's acquittal. It was attended by ranchers and cowboys from throughout the mountain country.

James B. O'Neil, in his book *They Die But Once*, wrote:

Pat Garrett and me was always friendly and several times I was partners with him in a business deal. I bought cattle for him and Cox in Old Mexico, below Ysleta. . . . I never believed Pat had any chance to fight when Wayne Braswell [*sic*] killed him. Cox had a mortgage on Garrett's property, and I'll always believe that Cox paid Braswell and the other feller to kill Garrett. . . . Old Cox was deadly afraid of Garrett; we all knowed that.

More and more it became evident that the invisible heads of this gigantic cattle ring had marked the territory's famed old sheriff for slaughter.

Governor Curry thought Brazil was "the victim of a conspiracy rather than the killer." Will Isaacs, who roomed with Brazil while he was out on bail and awaiting trial, recalled that he kept repeating the story of the shooting to himself, as if rehearsing it. One day, noting the doubt in Isaacs' face, he asked: "You don't believe me, do you?"

"Not a damn word of it," Isaacs replied, "but if you keep telling it over and over you will believe it yourself. You just ain't the killer type."

Brazil didn't deny it.

So few persons around Las Cruces believed Brazil's "confession" that even Garrett's friends bore him little enmity. Brazil showed good sense in one way. He never went around boasting that he was the slayer of the famous gunfighter who had downed Billy the Kid. Following the celebrated barbecue at Cox's ranch, he chose obscurity, ranching a while at Lordsburg, then in Arizona. No one seems to know what became of him or if he ever changed his story of what occurred on the road from Organ.

Jim Miller remained the bone of contention. Lorenzo D. Walters, who knew all the participants well, claimed, in his book *Tombstone's Yesterdays*, that Miller was "hired to come to New Mexico and kill Pat Garrett"—that Adamson was to cultivate the acquaintance of Garrett, then maneuver him into a spot where he could be dry-gulched by Miller. Ranger Captain John R. Hughes, who once saved Sheriff Frazer from assassination by Miller at Pecos, said that he had "obtained much information about the killing from unimpeachable sources" and that Miller was "close at hand when Garrett breathed his last."

Dee Harkey, in *Mean As Hell*, tells how Miller borrowed one of his horses from Joe Beasley, who was then working on his ranch in Roosevelt County, and rode it into the country where Garrett was slain. Miller returned the horse that night. The ride killed the horse.

When Harkey asked why the horse died, Beasley told him that Miller "rode him over and killed Pat Garrett," then told Beasley what he had done and stated that if he was ever indicted, he was going to expect Beasley to testify that he was at Harkey's ranch.

Harkey gave the information to Attorney General Hervey, but "Miller was never arrested."

Perhaps it was Harkey's story that took Hervey to Chicago to see his old friend Emerson Hough, author of *The Covered Wagon*, *The Story of the Cowboy*, *The Story of the Outlaw*, *North of '36*, and other books. After Brazil's acquittal, Hervey continued to work on what he believed to be an "unsolved criminal case." He had known Hough since his boyhood at Lincoln, when Hough was practicing law in Lincoln County. Hough had been a personal friend of Garrett, and Hervey urged him to offer a reward of one thousand dollars to any person willing to tell the truth about the Brazil-Garrett affair.

Hough said, "Jimmie, I know that outfit around the Organ Mountains. Garrett got killed trying to find out who killed Colonel Fountain, and you'll get killed trying to find out who killed Garrett if you don't go home and forget the whole thing."

Hervey took his advice.

After leaving the Harkey ranch, Miller presumably went back to Fort Worth. He was there off and on during the summer of 1908, gambling and dealing in real estate. The old indictment was pending against him at Ardmore, but no date for a trial had been set.

Toward the end of the year, he received a wire from El

Paso. His old friend Mannie Clements had been mysteriously slain in Tom Powers' Coney Island Saloon.

Miller swore to avenge Mannie's death, but he never got around to it. He had already been summoned to another job in Oklahoma. Trouble between the big ranchers in Pontotoc County, around Ada, had reached the burning point. Another man "needed killing." The fee was the sweetest ever offered him—two thousand dollars.

10. Murder at Rocky Branch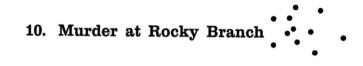

THE first white settlers to arrive on the site of Ada, Oklahoma, were the Daggs brothers, J. M. and J. B., who brought their families from Red River County, Texas, in 1890. Jeff Reed, who came with them driving their cattle, was so impressed with the locality that he hurried back to Red River County, disposed of his interests, and returned to Indian Territory. For about a year, the place was known as "Daggs Prairie." Then Reed established a small store. He hauled his initial stock from Denison, Texas, in an ox-drawn wagon. The store became a trading center for other whites and the Indians in the area and gave the settlement its first commercial importance. For the next two years, the settlement was called "Reed's Store." Other white families came; more businesses were established. In 1893, the settlement got a post office and was called "Ada," the name of Reed's eldest daughter.

During the late 1890's, the town was surveyed and platted, and a large area to the south was added for residential

92

expansion. The territory was being crisscrossed with new railroads in every direction, and the townsite promoters got busy. A contract for construction of the Missouri-Kansas-Texas, or "Katy," Railroad through Ada, Roff, and on to the Texas line was made in 1899. Lots were sold, more businesses sprang up, and two banks were established. In 1903, Ada was an ambitious city of three thousand inhabitants competing with Ardmore for the title, "Queen City of the Chickasaw Nation."

Like many other settlements, Ada, in the beginning, was without law enforcement except that provided by Indian Police and a few federal deputies passing through to the nearest court towns. In answer to an urgent request, Bob Nestor was assigned as resident United States deputy marshal.

Nestor wasn't much to look at. He was small of stature (not over five feet, six inches tall), horribly scarred from smallpox, and bowlegged from a lifetime in the saddle. But years of experience lay behind him. He worked out of Fort Smith, Arkansas, and Paris, Texas, rode a big horse with his Winchester strapped to the saddle, and carried twin six-shooters. Keen of eye and absolutely fearless, he always got his man.

His jail was a room in a local boarding house, equipped with a concrete post sunk through the center of the floor into the ground and two beds. If a prisoner had to be kept overnight before proceeding to the nearest federal jail, Nestor would shackle him to the post with a chain long enough that the man could reach the extra bed. He never lost a prisoner.

In 1902, Congress passed a bill establishing a federal court in Ada, and Nestor got some help.

The big jobs of the federal deputies were clearing out lot jumpers, running down horse and cattle thieves, and policing the whiskey joints that lined the South Canadian River on the border between Oklahoma Territory, where liquor was legal, and the Chickasaw and Seminole nations, where it was prohibited.

And there was always plenty of activity in Ada during the cotton season. Cotton was king in the surrounding areas. Laborers who drifted in to chop it in the spring picked it in the fall. Their wages and the proceeds from the sale of the crop increased the retail business. Ada became the cotton-marketing center of the Chickasaw Nation. It boasted five gins, a cottonseed oil mill, and a cotton compress. Its most influential and active civic leaders were cotton buyers, and hundreds of buyers flocked there from outside the territory.

During October and November, Main Street was jammed with wagons loaded with seed cotton and bales. Farmers often drove all night to be first in line at the gins in the morning. As soon as a wagon stopped on the street, the buyers, armed with sharp-bladed knives, swarmed over it, slashing the bagging and pulling out samples, examining them for color, grade, and length of staple. After a busy day, the many samples strewn in the street looked like patches of snow.

Gambling, dancing, and horse racing were the chief forms of entertainment, and arguments would build to a heated climax. For the thirsty gentry, Tin Top, Long Horn, Frosty, I-See, White Mule, and other so-called "territorial" beverages could be obtained in Ada. But most of the men headed for the oasis of saloons along the Canadian River, twelve to fifteen miles away.

There were sixty-two saloons and two licensed distilleries in Pottawatomie County to the north. While each town had its liquor merchants, the saloons that wrote history were along the Canadian at Keokuk Falls; Violet Springs;

Young's Crossing, due south of Sacred Heart Academy; and the Corner Crossing, in the very southeastern tip of the county. All these "line" settlements had their tinge of roughness. Several killings and robberies occurred around Young's, but this place was "a mischievous boy" compared to the infamous Corner.

In November, 1907, President Theodore Roosevelt signed the proclamation welding Oklahoma and Indian territories into one state. During the previous summer, with passage of the statehood bill assured by Congress, primary elections for state and local offices had been held. In Pontotoc County Robert Wimbish became the first county attorney, and Tom Smith, sheriff. On statehood day, oaths of office were administered to all officials. Ada was decorated with flags and bunting, bands played "Dixie" a dozen times, there was much oratory by both local and imported speakers, bonfires blazed on downtown streets and vacant lots, and everybody celebrated.

The town had arrived. It was spreading east and south. Three new additions had been sold.

The first of all civic clubs in Ada was the "25,000 Club." Organized in April, 1907, its aim was to "make Ada a city of 25,000." Its club room covered the entire second floor of the Cox-Greer store on east Main Street. Sumptuously furnished in leather-upholstered mission oak, it was the scene of much civic and social activity.

Late in November, the club listed Ada's major assets as a population of five thousand, five cotton gins, a cottonseed-oil mill, a cotton compress, an ice factory, a flour mill, machine shops, ice cream and canning factories, a brick and tile plant, a mammoth cement plant under construction, six loan and trust companies, two job printing offices, three newspapers, a light plant, a fire department, good schools, seven churches, three banks, and three railroads: the Katy, the Frisco, and the Oklahoma Central.

Most of the citizens had settled down to building a city of homes and legitimate enterprises, but there was another, troublesome group whose interests were outside the law. Despite Ada's progress and prosperity, the town had the reputation of being one of the last wild and woolly strongholds in the Southwest. The saloons across the Canadian had gone out of business with the coming of prohibition to the new state. Now, bootlegging dives lined the west end of Ada's Main Street. The patrons were old customers of the river saloons and hardened criminals who migrated to the town from all sections of the old territories.

Gunfighters with itchy trigger fingers boldly walked the streets in the employ of two powerful factions which had been feuding for years—one led by Angus A. Bobbitt, who held grazing leases from the Chickasaws south of the Canadian in Pontotoc County, the other by Joe Allen and Jesse West, who ran cattle in Pottawatomie County and on both sides of the river in the Seminole country and Pontotoc County to the east. Each hired as large a gang of gunmen as he could afford.

Just how tough Ada was is shown by the fact that during 1908 thirty-six murders were committed within the city limits or immediate vicinity.

Few cases were tried in the new courts. Despite the efforts of County Attorney Wimbish and Sheriff Tom Smith, killers with friends and money usually went free. Moman Pruiett, the famous criminal lawyer, living in nearby Pauls Valley, had all the business he could handle. In his flamboyant career he defended 342 accused murderers. Of this number, 304 escaped punishment. The remaining 38 were found guilty and were given sentences ranging from four years to life imprisonment. The only client of his ever sentenced to death was granted presidential clemency, and Pruiett often said he would quit practicing if ever he lost a client on the gallows. To the criminal element, Pruiett's name was sacred.

The Bobbitt-Allen-West feud had begun during the Canadian River saloon days. Bobbitt had pioneered the section in the 1880's, running longhorn herds on the site of Ada long before it became known as Daggs Prairie. He had contributed much to the building of the town and had served on one of its first boards of aldermen. Affectionately known as "Gus," he had a wife and four children and a host of friends in Ada, where he was a chapter Mason. He had long been an active participant in Democratic politics, both local and national. During President Cleveland's second administration, he had been the right-hand man of A. C. Cruce, the United States attorney at Ada. A Damon and Pythias friendship sprang up between Cruce and Bobbitt, and it was from Cruce that Bobbitt drew inspiration for his detestation of lawlessness. From 1895 to 1898 he had served as deputy under United States Marshal C. L. Stowe of the Southern District, and it was during this period that he made the bitter enemies who still feared and hated him.

Jesse West had been reared on a farm in Indian Territory. His first business venture was a store at Violet Springs. He soon tired of selling retail merchandise, however, and disposed of his entire stock and joined Joe Allen, a brother-in-law, in the cattle business. They prospered and decided to enter the whiskey trade along the Canadian. They acquired part of a fraction near the Corner and erected a rival saloon, operating it as a sideline and headquarters for their cattle interests.

A "fraction," in surveyor parlance, was the remainder of a quarter-section created by the meandering river. These parcels of land were not large enough to attract home-steaders who desired to farm, and for some time following the opening of the surplus lands of the Pottawatomie reservation in 1891, they remained public domain. However, they could be filed on and, once in possession of an individual, could be used for any legitimate purpose, including the sale of liquor.

A man named Bill Conner had acquired such a river-bottom fraction in the extreme southeastern corner of Pottawatomie County on the boundaries of Oklahoma Territory and the old Chickasaw and Seminole nations. In this jungle of cottonwoods, briars, plum thickets, and jack oaks, he had erected a saloon building forty feet inside the county line and about three hundred yards from the north bank of the river. It was the choice site for the lucrative "jug" trade among the Indians and outlaws that infested the bottomland, and with West and Allen almost in shooting distance, a feud was inevitable. After West and Allen destroyed his stock and fixtures, Conner was smart enough to sell to J. M. McCarty, now the owner of a third establishment, and leave him to fight it out. By this time, Conner's saloon had become known as "The Corner" because of its location.

McCarty was determined to save his investment despite the tactics of Allen and West. While Allen was the more positive of the two, West was the nervy one. He surrounded himself with many friends of his own character, brazen and fearless. McCarty, realizing the situation, imported two bodyguards from Texas—Frank Starr, the slayer of seven men, and George "Hookie" Miller, no relation of Deacon Jim. Miller had lost one hand, which had been replaced with a steel hook, and most of the digits of the second, but his remaining fingers were active with a six-shooter or Winchester. McCarty installed Hookie as bartender at the Corner.

West and Allen continued fighting for the liquor monopoly. First, they tried to trap McCarty into violating the laws against serving drinks on Sunday or to Indians or minors. Although every saloonkeeper along the river violated all these regulations, West and Allen were interested in "getting proof" only on McCarty.

Allen's son, Frank, posted himself just across the line in the Seminole Nation and sent a small boy after whiskey. After questioning the boy, Frank Starr rode over to deliver the whiskey in person, accompanied by Gus Bobbitt and Sherman Carter, former jailer at Ada.

As the three men approached the fence where the boy told them Allen was waiting, Starr called out: "Damn you, come get your whiskey!" Allen leaped from behind the fence and cut loose on Starr with a shotgun. Starr returned the fire and killed him. Bobbitt's testimony acquitted Starr.

Within a few months, Jesse West's boy was killed in a fight with a Negro. A West-Allen mob seized the Negro and tied him to a tree. They shot him in the knee, hoping that his cries might bring his companions to the scene. The blacks failed to respond, and the Negro was shot in the other knee. Still his companions refused to walk into the ambush.

Bobbitt championed the Negro and, when the man was later mysteriously slain, produced proof that he had met death at the hands of Jesse West. West was never charged with the killing. Afterward, he accused Bobbitt of rustling his cattle. Frank Starr espoused Bobbitt's cause and was soon joined by Hookie Miller.

Ed Hendricks, a half-blood Indian henchman of Jesse West, decided to kill Hookie Miller. Hendricks "came across

the river in his buggy, spoke insultingly to some men standing under a tree in front of the saloon, then walked rapidly
inside and asked Miller for a drink." Hookie, suspecting
trouble, reached under the bar as if for a bottle but came up
with a revolver. Hendricks fired, but missed. Hookie "shot
him twice with the revolver and once with a rifle after
Hendricks fell outside the door." Hookie was "held in jail
under bond for the salutary effect it would have upon
the situation."

Sheriff Grace and Deputy Will Carr of Pottawatomie
County made weekly visits to the bottoms, and Pottawatomie County Attorney S. P. Freeling warned the saloonkeepers that any further disorders or other law violations
would result in "the positive closing of their places." Mc-
Carty sold out to West and Allen, and Hookie Miller and
Frank Starr left the country.

The Corner now achieved the distinction of being the
"worst den of iniquity" in the territory, "where men of evil
name, fame and reputation congregated for the purpose of
cursing, drinking, shooting and performing unlawful acts."
The Shawnee *Daily Herald* of July 18, 1905, listed sixteen
cases of assault to kill, nine cases of murder, and eighty-one
liquor violations "directly traceable to the Corner since
last October." The "jug" trade increased. An Indian would
swap his saddle, pony, or even his rig for a supply of liquor.
The next day, another Indian would show up, claim the
article, and threaten to call federal officers. He would get the
article, but usually never got out of the country alive. In
December of the same year, an enthusiastic *Oklahoma State
Capital* journalist estimated that the Corner itself had been
"the scene of at least fifty murders" and that "the river
waters are like an abultion [*sic*] of blood."

County Attorney Freeling, over his own oath, supported

100

by affidavits of Bobbitt and others, filed a petition in district court and asked that a restraining order be granted. The West-Allen faction immediately filed a fistful of affidavits denying the allegations, and the failure of the county attorney to obtain sufficient evidence to the contrary caused the injunction to be dissolved.

Bobbitt withdrew from the conflict and tried to confine himself to his cattle interests south of the Canadian. One afternoon, West and Allen appeared in Ada, heavily armed. They cornered Bobbitt in a drug store, and it was only due to the presence of a number of local officials that they did not kill him. Later, Bobbitt armed himself with a Winchester and paraded the streets until they left town.

Finally, the public on both sides of the river got their fill of lawlessness and decided that Bobbitt or the others had to go. They looked the situation over from all angles. There were no halos about Gus Bobbitt's head, but he had proved himself to be a man of principle, so they threw the weight of respectability behind him.

Under this unified pressure, West and Allen sold their saloon interests. They moved their herds to Hemphill County, Texas, invested in cheap Panhandle lands, and again prospered. At a cattlemen's convention in Fort Worth in 1908, they boasted that they were worth $150,000.

But they hadn't forgotten how Bobbitt had run them out of Oklahoma. Like wounded rattlers, they would have been out of character not to make a last, deadly strike. The slaying of Pat Garrett in New Mexico, the major topic of conversation wherever cattlemen met, spurred their decision.

Toward the end of February, 1909, a frock-coated figure was seen riding through the timber near Bobbitt's home seven miles southwest of Ada.

On Saturday morning, February 27, Bobbitt went to Ada

101

to transact some business. At five-thirty in the evening, he started home in a wagon loaded with sacks of meal cake. A neighbor, Bob Ferguson, jogged along behind in another wagon similarly loaded. Here is Ferguson's prelude to what happened:

We reached Simmons Crossing about sundown. We were going south on the regular Roff-Ada road. The sun hadn't gone when we reached Rocky Branch. After we crossed the creek and passed the corner of a field there, we met a man on horseback.

He was going north, on the east side of the road. He spoke to Mr. Bobbitt; he didn't speak to me. He was riding a brown mare, about fifteen hands high, of rough appearance, sides saddle shaved and a white spot on the forehead. Shod all around. She was branded "J," with a scar on the left thigh. I noticed a long object tied behind the saddle wrapped in what I thought was a slicker, but more like buggy curtain material, the white on the outside. I didn't pay much attention to the man. He wore a striped tie and white collar, and a white handkerchief around his neck. He had another handkerchief in his hand, held up to his face, wiping his left eye as he passed us.

After we met this rider, we left the road and entered the northeast corner of the field through a wire gate. I looked back and saw this man ride over the top of the hill to the right. It was past sundown by then.

In a dusky hollow half a mile north of Bobbitt's ranch house, the double barrel of a shotgun was thrust through the crotch of a big elm in a clump of trees. The wagons approached slowly. Finally, Bobbitt drew abreast of the trees beside the road.

The shotgun blazed twice. The first load of buckshot struck him in the lower limbs. As he reared up on the meal sacks, the second charge tore into his left side at the vest pocket. He uttered a low cry, "Oh, God!" and toppled head-first from the wagon. His team broke and ran.

Ferguson wheeled his wagon from the road and leaped down from his seat to shelter on the opposite side. In a moment, the stranger he had seen earlier on the trail rode out of the trees and galloped away in the dusk.

Ferguson unhitched one of his horses, caught Bobbitt's team, and rode to the ranch for help. Mrs. Bobbitt had heard the shooting and was standing on the porch. Ferguson told the horrified woman that Gus had been shot. Within minutes, she was at the side of her husband, trying to stop the flow of blood, while Ferguson rode to telephone officers and a doctor.

Bobbitt lived nearly an hour after being shot. The Ada *News* recorded:

Lying there in the moonlight, with only streaking shadows from the old tree which had sheltered his murderer to transgress the hallowed scene, he requested his wife to place his head in her lap. He kept his coat buttoned over his wound and told his wife not to talk to him, as he wanted to take what time he had left talking to her. . . He said he did not know his assassin, but thought he had been hired by some of his old enemies. . . . He gave directions as to the disposition of his property, and made his will, specifying that $1,000 go as a reward for the arrest and conviction of his killer.

11. Rope's End

ADA, hard-bitten town that it was, was stirred to a frenzy. Had the assassin faced Bobbitt in the open and shot it out, the killing would have attracted no more attention than many others. But the cowardly ambush of a man going peacefully home to his family was more than even its worst citizens could stomach.

Officers hurried to the scene but accomplished nothing that night. On Sunday morning, hundreds of persons gathered in Ada's 25,000 Club rooms to organize a full-scale hunt. They subscribed seven hundred dollars for expenses and elected an executive committee to administer the funds and direct the pursuit. Then every able-bodied man with a gun set out to find the murderer.

On a hill above Rocky Branch, they discovered where the killer had entered a pasture after cutting through the fence. They followed the tracks north across the prairie until they reached the Parkell switch on the Frisco. Here the killer had cut two fences. At the second fence he had lost his wire

104

cutters and set fire to the grass trying to find them. The posse recovered the wire cutters but lost the trail farther north where it turned through a gate into a public road. They thought the killer had boarded a Frisco train. But another group who talked with John Rollins, who farmed on the railroad four miles south of Ada, received different information. Rollins had seen the killer shortly after dark. "The moon was up bright, and he came right up on me, dressed in his black coat and riding that brown mare. I was at the spring by the old waste house across the road west of here, watering my cow. He stopped to water the mare, then saw me, and took off down the hollow in a lope."

The pursuers picked up Miller's tracks at the spring. The trail led north again, above Ada, then turned northeast along the railroad. By midafternoon, some twenty miles farther, the posse reached the farm of twenty-four-year-old John Williamson, south of Francis, where they found the mare. Her shoes had been removed, but the astute investigators soon located them hidden under the floor of Williamson's kitchen. The shoes "corresponded to a point" with the tracks leading from the scene of the murder.

Williamson denied that the mare had been out of his pasture. Then somebody punched him in the face, blood ran from his nose, and he told them a man had paid him twenty dollars for the use of his pony.

"What man?"

"I don't know."

Somebody else seized his arm and twisted it. "You'd better talk!"

Williamson turned pale. "I can't tell—he'll kill me!"

The man twisted harder. "If he don't, we will! What man?"

Williamson looked around nervously. What he saw in the

faces of the posse turned him limp, and he started babbling: "I had nothing to do with it! I swear! I want to see the sheriff—I'll tell all I know!"

The posse took him to jail at Ada. That evening, he dictated a statement to Sheriff Tom Smith and County Attorney Wimbish.

The man they wanted was his uncle, Jim Miller. "He came to my house last Monday," Williamson began:

He was in a buggy with a boy named Oscar Peeler. I didn't talk to Peeler. Uncle Jim came in the house, and Peeler stayed in the buggy.

Uncle Jim asked to borrow my pony. He claimed to be on a land deal, to trade land for cattle, down about Roff—he didn't say for certain where—and take them down to a ranch about Ardmore. I told him I didn't see how I could do without my pony, that I needed her for farming, and he told me, "If I make this deal for the cattle, I'll hire you to help drive them to the ranch and give you a steady job; you will make more out of that than farming." He said he would pay me good for the use of my pony and would be back in a few days. I told him all right.

I saw him again in Francis, on Saturday. Peeler was there. He had another man in the buggy with him. I don't know his name. He gave Miller some money. . . .

I next saw my pony about ten o'clock that night. I had gone to bed. Uncle Jim rode up and hollered "Hello." I went out to feed the mare. She looked to be sweating, the saddle blanket was wet. When she got through eating, I put her in the pasture and came back and sat in the house with Uncle Jim. He said he was sleepy and had a headache. I told him maybe it would help if he ate something and drank some coffee. He drank the coffee and ate a few bites and went to bed.

He didn't sleep very good. I heard him a time or two in the night, blowing his nose. He got up about sunup, ate

106

breakfast. I asked if he had made the deal for the cattle; he said, "No, but I made a bigger piece of money." I asked him how, and he didn't answer. He asked me to take him to Sasakwa. I saddled my bay horse and brown mare, and asked him again how he made that piece of money. He said, "I killed a man."

He said there were some other fellows behind it, and if I talked, they would hurt me. I asked who he'd killed, and he said, "Bobbitt." He said, "Don't you say anything about it, or you're liable to get killed." He told me that three or four times during the trip.

When we got to Sasakwa, he went to the depot and I didn't see him anymore. He gave me $2.00 for carrying him over there, and told me to kill the mare. I told him no, I needed her to farm with. He said, "Then take her to another pasture or something, and take them shoes off her." I took the shoes off that day.

Williamson was held as a material witness under $2,500 bond. The investigation quickened to a climax.

The depot agent at Sasakwa remembered a man of Miller's description buying a ticket Sunday morning to Ardmore. Believing that Miller might still be in that city, Sheriff Smith wired Chief of Police Buck Garrett, then boarded a train to Ardmore to help make the apprehension.

Chief Garrett knew Miller from his days in the federal jail during 1907. He learned that Miller had arrived there on the Monday morning following Bobbitt's slaying and that early in February he had stayed several days at a local rooming house.

The landlady told officers:

I left before Christmas and was gone about five weeks. Miller was here when I got home. He had a grip and a gun. It was a shotgun, done up in oil cloth—a light-colored cloth with tan straps around it. He left the gun with me from that morning until in the afternoon, then came and got it. He was in a buggy then, with a young fellow named Peeler.

Peeler worked on a farm seven miles west of Ardmore. Thinking that Miller might be in hiding there, Chief Garrett and a posse of Ardmore officers surrounded the farmhouse. They did not find Miller, but they arrested nineteen-year-old Oscar Peeler.

Peeler admitted his acquaintance with Miller. "I knew him in Fort Worth about a year ago. He hired me to drive him to Ada, then I came home. I don't know where he is now."

A warrant for Miller's arrest was wired to Fort Worth, and Sheriff Smith returned Peeler to Ada.

Peeler languished in jail, refusing to talk even after Williamson identified him as the man he had seen with Miller at his home and in Francis. Finally, County Attorney Wimbish charged him with complicity in the slaying of Bobbitt. The charge of murder quickly loosened Peeler's tongue. He sent for Wimbish, and gave a full confession.

I got $50 to bring Mr. Miller up here. He said he had a land deal and was dealing in cattle. After we got here, he said that he wanted to kill this man Bobbitt. I got scared and told him, if he wanted to do that, I was going home. He said, "We'll both go back in a day or two," and he gave me another $25. I got my money from Jesse West. Miller said the money came from Jesse West.

Two men had hired Miller to "exterminate" Bobbitt—West and Joe Allen. They had paid Miller two thousand dollars for the killing and three thousand dollars to be used in the event of his capture. It was "just a matter of business" with Deacon Jim—sort of a lark into an area where murder had been as easy as shooting ducks in a rain barrel. He had never seen Bobbitt before in his life.

The money, claimed Peeler, who maintained that his only role was to haul Miller from place to place and finally to Francis for the payoff, was in cash and carried by an intermediary to avert suspicion. The intermediary was a local livestock dealer and old friend of West and Allen from the Corner saloon days—Berry B. Burrell.

"Burrell spotted Bobbitt for Miller," Peeler said. "He saw Bobbitt loading up with meal cake and went out and told Miller that Bobbitt was coming."

Burrell was a native of Parker County, Texas. He had come to Oklahoma in territorial days, serving for a time as cashier of a bank at El Reno. Later, he had resided at Fort Worth, where he became a speculator in livestock. In 1905, he had moved to Ada, making it headquarters for his trips to all parts of the state buying cattle and hogs for the northern Texas markets. He was widely known among commission men and farmers with whom he dealt. Unmarried, he roomed at a downtown hotel.

Sheriff Smith didn't find him at the hotel. Burrell was in Fort Worth to attend a fat stock show. Smith wired Tarrant County authorities. On March 12, the day the show opened, Burrell was arrested by two deputy sheriffs while talking with friends on Fort Worth's Main Street. He "made light of the charges against him" and waived extradition. He knew nothing of Williamson's statement or of Peeler's confession until he reached Ada.

Tarrant County authorities learned that Miller had been seen north of Fort Worth in the Trinity bottoms. A few days later, their informant told them where Miller was hiding. On the afternoon of March 30, Deputy Sheriffs Tom Snow and Sid Higgins arrested him at a farmhouse in the brakes of

Dozier Creek, a few miles southwest of Hicks. Miller surrendered peacefully, although a Winchester rifle, two revolvers, and a shotgun in an oilcloth case lay in the room that he occupied.

"I've never given any officer trouble who came after me," Deacon Jim explained politely. "I prefer to take my chances in court."

The deputies took him to Fort Worth, where Smith and George Culver, Ada's chief of police, waited to return him to Oklahoma.

Miller asked that he be allowed to carry his revolvers in his grip. The officers denied the request.

"Well, I'll waive extradition and go face those people up there anyway. I had no connection with this killing," he said.

He was lodged in the Ada jail on April 1. Only West and Allen remained to be taken into custody. County Attorney Wimbish knew that, unlike Burrell and Miller, they would resist any attempt to remove them to Oklahoma. A telegram went over the wires to Jesse West at Canadian, Texas: "You and Joe come to Ada at once. Need $10,000. Miller."

The ruse worked. West and Allen boarded a train for Oklahoma immediately. On the night of April 6, on instructions from Wimbish, they were arrested in Oklahoma City by Detectives William Slaton and Robert Moore as they exchanged greetings with their lawyer, who had just stepped off the northbound Katy from Ada.

At police headquarters, they "talked quite a little and begged not to be taken to Pontotoc County."

West told Detective Moore: "We didn't kill Bobbitt. The only reason, we never got a chance. But they will kill us if you take us to Ada. They will shoot us through the train windows, or through the jail doors—any way they can."

The prisoners were booked into jail for the night. The

next morning, they were removed to Ada, under heavy guard, by State Officer Todd Warden.

At last, all principals in the Bobbitt case were behind bars—Burrell, West, Allen, and Miller. The preliminary hearing was held Friday afternoon, April 16, before Justice of the Peace H. J. Brown. It was the most unusual court proceeding in Oklahoma history. Before the trial began, Justice Brown issued the following edict:

The State of Oklahoma
          vs.   No. —
Jim Miller, et al, Defendants
                    Order of the Court

In the Justice Court in and for Ada Township, Pontotoc County, Oklahoma, before Hon. H. J. Brown, Justice of the Peace.

Now on this, the 15th day of April, A.D. 1909, the Court of its own motion doth order that *no reporter for any newspaper be allowed in the court room during the trial of the above styled cause for the purpose of taking the testimony introduced in the trial of the same.* It is further ordered that *none of the testimony taken in the above styled cause shall be published in any newspaper in Pontotoc County.* And it is further the order of this Court that the stenographer employed by the state to take the testimony herein *shall return to this Court the original transcript of said testimony, when the same has been by her transcribed, together with any and all copies of the same which she may make or cause to be made in transcribing the same for her original notes of same taken on the trial of this cause.*

The Court further orders the officers of this Court, including the Sheriff, Bailiffs, Constables, Deputy Sheriffs, Deputy Constables and all appointees of the Sheriff or any Deputy in attendance of this Court to *search any and all persons they may see fit or may deem necessary, before or*

111

after any such person or persons enter the Court room, for any weapons of any descriptions whatever.

Given under my hand this the 15th day of April, A.D. 1909. [author's italics.]

Local newspapers had avoided elaborate coverage of Bobbitt's assassination and co-operated fully with officers throughout the hunt for his slayer for reasons set forth in an Ada *News* editorial of March 4:

The death, the manner of its hellish accomplishment, and the impression the extraordinary personality of the victim has wrought on the minds of the public during all the years of his life in our midst have so influenced the senses of our people that many words have been spoken and many scenes enacted which are portentious of much in the future, entirely enough if related and described to fill all the columns of the *News*, and of such nature that if published the tenseness of the public's agitation would probably increase manifold.

The editor who achieves success for his paper must adhere to the policy and principles of publishing the news, and it is always agreed that the detail with which it is worked out should be commensurate with the interests of its reception.

But the *News'* consideration of its function is absolutely secondary to its consideration of the wishes of Mr. Bobbitt's close friends and those who are leading in the undertaking to apprehend the assassin and accomplices; and, agreeable to their wishes, the reports of the clues found, the general evidence in hand and the names of the parties suspicioned remains censored from this paper.

The feeling of the community and the sympathy which prevailed was better estimated by the *News* on Thursday afternoon, March 1, when the remains of Bobbitt were laid to rest:

A great congregation of his friends assembled near the

Masonic Hall at 2:30 awaiting the conclusion of the preparation of the Masons for the funeral march and awaiting the arrival of that part of the burial party accompanying the relatives with the remains from the country home. . . .

When the march from the Masonic Hall of the large procession led by the Masons who were more immediately escorting the corpse and closely following relatives had begun and proceeded through the main streets where business had suspended and closed doors, a most impressive, even imposing scene was presented, one surely remindful to the coldest heart and dullest sensibility that the people of Pontotoc County are firmly pledged to the support of law and order and deeply regardful of whom it has been said "He led all in its preservation when the sacrifice of its peace and dignity were most imminent. . . ."

The ceremony and the incidents of the burial were affecting and during the performance of the last sad rites there was a mute sob from many a brave and loyal heart and a plentitude of tears from many a loved one whose grief is unbounded.

So the *News* accepted Justice Brown's edict philosophically:

Verily the impediments to maintaining a daily newspaper in a small town increase. . . . We had hoped to give our readers a stenographic report of the testimony. This would have been a good stroke from the standpoint of journalism, and while our readers would have appreciated the full proceedings, the *News* is not ruffled. . . . Not for a moment would we insist on following a policy which would in all likelihood result in the impediment of justice or in bringing about a condition by which the court would be placed at a disadvantage from any standpoint, or the county involved in additional expense.

The town waited.

113

Peeler and Williamson turned state's evidence. For their own safety, they were transferred to the Pottawatomie County jail at Tecumseh. Burrell, Allen, West, and Miller were ordered held for district court trial without bail. To Ada citizens, it was tantamount to positive guilt.

West, Allen, and Burrell knew the temper of the community, but Miller laughed at their fears. He dressed in stiff-bosomed white shirts, shaved twice daily, had fresh linen sent up for his bed each morning, ordered porterhouse steaks from a nearby restaurant, and tipped the jailer with five-dollar bills. He wanted all and sundry to know that "royalty was being unjustly detained and embarrassed." Thoroughly familiar with the ways of frontier courts, he knew what money and influence could do.

So did Ada.

The people grew ominously quiet. They saw hundreds of telegrams and letters pour in, lauding Miller's character, and a score of prominent Texas and New Mexico cattlemen come forward to praise him as a sterling citizen. Impressed by his arrogance, West and Allen placed an additional ten thousand dollars at his disposal.

Miller chuckled. He wisecracked about the stupidity of the town in general and announced that he had employed the famous criminal lawyer, Moman Pruiett, to defend him and his partners.

It looked as though Deacon Jim was about to execute another legal farce.

Shortly after 2:00 A.M., Sunday, April 19, a mob of "forty masked men" forced open the doors to the county jail. They beat two guards over the head with pistol barrels and bound them with baling wire. Then they took Burrell, Allen, West, and Miller from their cells.

West was the only member of the quartet who resisted.

114

He was quickly beaten into submission. With blood streaming from his face and head, he was dragged with the others down the murky alley to an abandoned livery barn behind the jail.

The mob worked rapidly and quietly. The prisoners' hands were bound tightly behind them and the first man to swing from the rafters was Jesse West. Next in quick succession came Allen and Burrell. The mob saved Miller until last and for several minutes tried to get him to confess his crimes.

"Just let the record show that I've killed fifty-one men," he said.

He was absolutely without fear. He had lived that way and he could die that way.

Calmly, he removed his diamond ring and asked that it be sent to his wife in Fort Worth. Next, he handed his diamond shirt stud to one of the lynchers to be given to the jailer for his kindness.

As they placed the noose around his neck, he said to the mob leaders: "I'd like to have my coat. I don't want to die naked."

Even in his last moments Deacon Jim must have believed that so long as he wore his black coat he was invincible.

The mob refused his request. "If I can't have my coat, then how about my hat?" he asked.

Somebody jammed his hat on the side of his head. "I'm ready now," Miller laughed. "You couldn't kill me otherwise. Let 'er rip!"

The rope over the rafter jerked and Miller was left with feet dangling.

When the body stopped quivering, one man lifted the black coat and draped it over Deacon Jim's sagging shoulders. "It won't help him now," he said.

The ghastly business done, the mob dispersed in the night through a light drizzle of rain that had begun to fall.

The identities of the members of the lynch mob were never established. No one really cared. Too long had the town's growth been thwarted under the trigger fingers of the most cold-blooded killers in the Southwest. They had brought the curtain down with gruesome solemnity on an outlaw era.

Bibliography

Public Records

Miller v. *State*, Cause No. 3283, *Texas Criminal Appeals*, Vol. 18, p. 232.

Records of County Attorney, Pottawatomie County, Tecumseh, Indian Territory, 1905–1907.

Records of County Attorney, Pottawatomie County, Ada, Oklahoma, 1909.

State of Oklahoma v. *Jim Miller*, et al., *Defendants*, (case number not assigned), Justice of the Peace Court, Ada Township, Pontotoc County, Oklahoma, April 15–16, 1909.

State of Texas v. *Barney Riggs*, Case No. 2068, *District Court Minutes*, El Paso County, Texas, Vol. 9, p. 325.

State of Texas v. *G. A. Frazer*, Case No. 190, District Court, Reeves County, Texas, March 5, 1895.

State of Texas v. *G. A. Frazer*, Case No. 1110, *District Court Minutes*, Mitchell County, Texas, Vol. 1, p. 305.

State of Texas v. *G. A. Frazer*, Case No. 1789, *District*

117

Court Minutes, El Paso County, Texas, Vol. 8, p. 425.

State of Texas v. *M. Q. Hardin*, Case No. 150, District Court, Reeves County, Texas, September Term, 1893.

State of Texas v. *J. B. Miller*, Case No. 238, District Court, Reeves County, Texas, September Term, 1896.

Statement of John Williamson, subscribed and sworn to before H. J. Brown, Justice of the Peace, Ada Township, Pontotoc County, Oklahoma, 1909.

Statement of Oscar Peeler, subscribed and sworn to before H. J. Brown, Justice of the Peace, Ada Township, Pontotoc County, Oklahoma, 1909.

Newspapers

Ada (Oklahoma) *Daily Democrat*, February–May, 1909.

Ada (Oklahoma) *Daily News*, March–May, 1909.

Ada (Oklahoma) *Weekly Democrat*, February–April, 1909.

Ada (Oklahoma) *Weekly News*, February–April, 1909.

Chickasaw Capital (Tishomingo, Oklahoma), August, 1906; April, 1909.

Daily Ardmoreite (Ardmore, Oklahoma), August, 1906; February–May, 1909; August–October, 1910.

Daily Oklahoman (Oklahoma City, Oklahoma), February–April, 1909.

Dallas (Texas) *Morning News*, February, 1909.

Durant (Oklahoma) *Daily News*, August, 1906.

El Paso (Texas) *Daily Herald*, February–April, 1908; April, 1909; December, 1909.

El Paso (Texas) *Times*, April, 1894; March–April, 1895; August, 1895; September, 1896; May, 1897; July, 1910.

Fort Worth (Texas) *Record*, March–April, 1909.

Fort Worth (Texas) *Register*, June–July, 1897.

Galveston (Texas) *News*, September, 1896.

Guthrie (Oklahoma) *Daily Leader*, March–May, 1909.

Hobart (Oklahoma) *Republican,* November–December, 1906.

Houston (Texas) *Chronicle*, April, 1909.

Lawton (Oklahoma) *Daily News-Republican*, February, 1909.

Lexington (Oklahoma) *Leader*, April, 1909.

Milburn (Oklahoma) *News*, August, 1906.

New Mexico Sentinel (Albuquerque, New Mexico), April, 1939.

Oklahoma State Capital (Oklahoma City, Oklahoma), April, 1898; July, 1903; July, 1905; December, 1905; September–December, 1906; January, 1907; May–July, 1909; August, 1910.

Shawnee (Oklahoma) *Daily Herald*, July, 1905.

Shawnee (Oklahoma) *News*, April, 1909.

Tucson (Arizona) *Citizen*, November, 1887.

Books

Abernathy, John R. (Jack). *In Camp with Roosevelt; or, the Life of John R. (Jack) Abernathy*. Oklahoma City, The Times-Journal Publishing Co., 1933.

Bartholomew, Ed. *The Biographical Album of Western Gunfighters*. Houston, The Frontier Press of Texas, 1958.
————. *Kill or Be Killed: A Record of Violence in the Early Southwest*. Houston, The Frontier Press of Texas, 1953.

Biles, J. Hugh. *The Early History of Ada*. Ada, Okla., published by the Oklahoma State Bank in commemoration of its fiftieth anniversary, 1954.

Burns, Walter Noble. *The Saga of Billy the Kid*. Garden City, N.Y., Doubleday, Page & Company, 1926.

Casey, Robert J. *The Texas Border and Some Borderliners:*

119

A Chronicle and a Guide. Indianapolis and New York, The Bobbs-Merrill Company, Inc., 1950.

Cunningham, Eugene. *Triggernometry: A Gallery of Gunfighters.* New York, The Press of the Pioneers, Inc., 1934.

Ford, John Salmon. *Rip Ford's Texas.* Ed. with introduction and commentary by Stephen B. Oates. Austin, University of Texas Press, 1963.

Garrett, Patrick Floyd. *The Authentic Life of Billy, the Kid.* Biographical foreword by Jarvis P. Garrett. Albuquerque, Horn & Wallace, Publishers, Inc., 1964.

Gibson, A. M. *The Life and Death of Colonel Albert Jennings Fountain.* Norman, University of Oklahoma Press, 1965.

Greer, James Kimmins. *Colonel Jack Hays: Texas Frontier Leader and California Builder.* New York, E. P. Dutton & Company, Inc., 1952.

Haley, J. Evetts. *Charles Goodnight: Cowman & Plainsman.* Norman, University of Oklahoma Press, 1949.

———. *Jeff Milton: A Good Man With a Gun.* Norman, University of Oklahoma Press, 1948.

Hardin, John Wesley. *The Life of John Wesley Hardin, From the Original Manuscript As Written by Himself.* Seguin, Texas, Smith & Moore, 1896.

Harkey, Dee. *Mean As Hell.* Albuquerque, University of New Mexico Press, 1948.

Henning, H. B., ed. *George Curry, 1861–1947: An Autobiography.* Albuquerque, University of New Mexico Press, 1958.

Hughes, W. J. *Rebellious Ranger: Rip Ford and the Old Southwest.* Norman, University of Oklahoma Press, 1964.

Keleher, William A. *The Fabulous Frontier: Twelve New Mexico Items.* Santa Fe, The Rydal Press, 1945.

————. *Violence in Lincoln County, 1869–1881: A New Mexico Item*. Albuquerque, University of New Mexico Press, 1957.

Knight, Oliver. *Fort Worth: Outpost on the Trinity*. Norman, University of Oklahoma Press, 1953.

Kupper, Winifred. *The Golden Hoof: The Story of the Sheep of the Southwest*. New York, Alfred A. Knopf, 1945.

MacCreary, Henry. *A Story of Durant, "Queen of Three Valleys."* Durant, Okla., 1945.

Martin, Jack. *Border Boss: Captain John R. Hughes, Texas Ranger*. San Antonio, The Naylor Company, Publishers, 1942.

Metz, Leon Claire. *John Selman: Texas Gunfighter*. New York, Hastings House, Publishers, 1966.

Nordyke, Lewis. *John Wesley Hardin: Texas Gunman*. New York, William Morrow & Company, 1957.

O'Connor, Richard. *Pat Garrett: A Biography of the Famous Marshal and the Killer of Billy the Kid*. Garden City, N.Y., Doubleday & Company, Inc., 1960.

O'Neil, James Bradas. *They Die But Once: The Story of a Tejano*. New York, Knight Publications, Inc., 1935.

Pruiett, Moman. *Moman Pruiett: Criminal Lawyer*. Oklahoma City, Harlow Publishing Corp., 1944.

Raymond, Dora Neill. *Captain Lee Hall of Texas*. Norman, University of Oklahoma Press, 1940.

Sonnichsen, C. L. *Ten Texas Feuds*. Albuquerque, University of New Mexico Press, 1957.

————. *Tularosa: Last of the Frontier West*. New York, The Devin-Adair Company, 1960.

Walters, Lorenzo D. *Tombstone's Yesterdays*. Tucson, Acme Printing Company, 1928.

Webb, Walter Prescott. *The Texas Rangers: A Century of*

Frontier Defense. Boston and New York, Houghton Mifflin Company, 1935.

Articles in Periodicals

Clark, Neil M. "Close Calls," *The American Magazine*, Vol. CVII, No. 1 (January, 1929).

Hope, Welborn. "Our Badmen Were Good," *Sunday Oklahoman*, January 14, 1951.

———. "End of the Old Southwest," *Sunday Oklahoman*, March 4, 1951.

———. "Wild, Woolly Southwest Died With Four Men Strung Up In Barn in 1909," Tulsa *Citizen-News*, Thursday, March 28, 1962.

———. "Before Wild Southwest Was Tamed, Lynch Mob Dealt Swift Justice," Tulsa *Citizen-News*, Thursday, April 26, 1962.

Hunt, Frazier. "The Tall Slayer of Billy the Kid," *Argosy*, Vol. 331, No. 6 (December, 1950).

Hough, Emerson. "The American Six-Shooter," *Outing Magazine*, Vol. LIII, No. 4 (January, 1909).

McDaniel, Ruel. "Killer For Hire—51 Victims," *Crime Detective*, November, 1946.

Secrest, William B. "The Last Ride," *True West*, Vol. 14, No. 3 (January–February, 1967).

Pamphlets

Fortson, John. *Pott County and What Has Come of It: A History of Pottawatomie County*. Shawnee, Okla., Pottawatomie County Historical Society, Herald Printing Company, 1936.

Gill, Ed. *The Early Days of Milburn: A Chronicle, 1901–1920*. Tishomingo, Okla., Capital-Democrat Press, 1960.

Leftwich, Bill. *Tracks Along the Pecos*. Pecos, Texas, Pecos Press, 1957.

Scanland, John Milton. *The Life of Pat F. Garrett and the Taming of the Border Outlaws: A History of the "Gun Men" and Outlaws, and a Life Story of the Greatest Sheriff of the Southwest*. El Paso, Press of the Southwestern Printing Co., 1908.

Index

125